CONTENTS

Acknowledgments

The opportunity to write books with my father has been one of the most unpredictable yet rewarding experiences. So, first of all, I would like to acknowledge all of the hard work my father has done just to get me to this point in life. Of course, without his research and creativity, this book would not have been possible either.

My father and I would both like to think our wives, Nancy Murrie and Seung Ah Lee, for being our first audience. Without their hard work and patience, we would never have been able to find a second audience to read this book.

We would also like to think our agent, Jessica Regel (along with everyone else at the Jean V. Naggar Literary Agency) who was the first to believe in our writing and whose work to get us published has truly been second to none. We would also like to thank our editors at Adams Media, Meredith O'Hayre and Katie Corcoran-Lytle, who demonstrated incredible levels of dedication and patience (especially patience) during the writing process.

And a special thank you to Dr. Tobias Gibson, Assistant Professor of Political Science at Westminster College, in Fulton, MO for his help and ideas on several entries.

Because second place is more than just the first loser

THE FIRST BOOK OF
SECONDS

220 *of the Most* **Random**, **Remarkable**, **Respectable** (*and* **REGRETTABLE**) Runners-Up *and Their* **Almost Claims to Fame**

Fact: People give Mount Everest more credit than it deserves. When it comes right down to it, there isn't that much separating Everest from K2, the world's second-tallest mountain. Sure, K2 is only 28,251 feet tall next to Everest's 29,029 feet, but if you fall, the outcome will most likely be the same.

Fact: When it comes to plastic surgery, breast augmentation wins the award for "Most Commonly Performed" by a nose. The second-most -common surgery? Rhinoplasty. As in nose jobs. About 256,000 nose jobs, or "nose reshapings," as the formerly big-schnozzed prefer to call them, are performed each year. Fortunately, most are performed to fix deviated septums—and if you believe that we'll tell you another one.

Fact: The second-largest land animal, the Asian elephant, is a big creature at 11,000 pounds, 9½ feet. But it is downright tiny compared to its larger cousin, the African elephant, which lumbers in at 27,000 pounds, 27½ feet. Wonder if it has an inferiority complex?

TOP-NOTCH
TRIVIA
—FOR THE—
RUNNER-UP
IN ALL OF US

MATTHEW MURRIE & STEVE MURRIE

Aadamsmedia
Avon, Massachusetts

Published by Adams Media,
a division of F+W Media, Inc.
57 Littlefield Street,
Avon, MA 02322. U.S.A.
www.adamsmedia.com

ISBN 10: 1-4405-0752-X
ISBN 13: 978-1-4405-0752-6
eISBN 10: 1-4405-1067-9
eISBN 13: 978-1-4405-1067-0

Printed in the United States of America.

10   9   8   7   6   5   4   3   2   1

Library of Congress Cataloging-in-Publication Data
is available from the publisher.

Interior image credits

clown, tickets, ice cream, mesopatamia © istockphoto/Aaltazar; teapot, coffee © istockphoto/Mr_Vector; stick figures © istockphoto/danleap; award, dog, cat, fish, syringe, gun, fire, knife, tee/ball, glove, caddy, golf course © istockphoto/roccomontoya; tv, film reel, record, music notes, microphone © istockphoto/runeer; computer, record, phone, remote, calculator © istockphoto/molotovcoketail; rocket, UFO, torch, column, field goal, basketball hoop, baseball © istockphoto/bubaone; marionette © istockphoto/Vallentin; animals © istockphoto/filo; car, bike, train, bus © istockphoto/hemmo; farm animals © istockphoto/Ace_Create; fruits and vegetables © istockphoto/cidepix; peanuts © istockphoto/pukrufus; nuclear, coal, lightning © istockphoto/Kami-Gami; white house © istockphoto/slowgogo; empire state building © istockphoto/blamb; yacht © istockphoto/Leontura; flag, running shoe, helmet © istockphoto/miniature; jeep, hot air balloon, boat plane © istockphoto/kkonkle; horse © istockphoto/Xonkdesign; Moses © istockphoto/toniton; impeach © istockphoto/BenThomasPhoto; mummy © istockphoto/KeithBishop

Clouds, pecan, mask, popsicle, pill bottle, beet, ketchup, chocolate, stars, Tuvalu, sequoia, peace sign, sun, comet, bungee jump, Spirit of Freedom, Callisto, cryovolcano, telescope, dinosaur, canopus, balloon, Humongous Fungus, Ogallala, Monkey Puzzle tree, rain bucket, Challenger Deep, exploding soda, Marilyn Monroe, Stanley Cup, NBA trophy, amboni, recycle, shoe, glasses by Elisabeth Lariviere.

All other images © 123RF.

Introduction

What's happened to good, ole number two? One is the loneliest number—it even has a song! And three can be company or charmed, how great is that? Two? Number two is reserved for the smallest room in the house. Typically, the only thing that comes to most people's minds when they hear about number two stinks. *The First Book of Seconds* is here to change all of that.

If you think seconds are second class, then you obviously know number two about seconds. Why don't you take a second to consider:

The second hand on the clock is the one that ticks.

Your second wind is the one that makes you a winner.

A second nature comes naturally.

The second day of work or school is when things really begin.

Second thoughts tend to be the more rational ones. Yet, a second mortgage is the costly one.

Second semester? Time to get serious, unless you want to take the class a second time.

A second kiss knows what it's doing.

A second date heats things up.

Second cousins are the first ones you get to kiss.

And with the second trimester comes the first kicks.

If you're fortunate enough to have a second home, it's most likely the relaxing one.

Second chances? Who doesn't need one?

In fact, second editions set first mistakes straight.

And, lastly, the Second Coming, your second incarnation, or simply your final seconds is what happens next.

Or, maybe you're a second child, with your second spouse, or you're the second to carry a family name. You could be living in your second country or filling your plate with second helpings. No matter what, seconds are virtually unavoidable—and what a shame if they weren't.

And that's just for starters. So, whether you are hungry for facts or ready for seconds, *The First Book of Seconds* is here to serve them up. Just wait until you see what you discover when you dig past the first and find a second to uncover. With seconds covering such a multitude of human emotions, experiences, accomplishments, and thoughts, you have to wonder:

Why do we *ever* stop at firsts?

PART 1

Pop Culture Seconds

In an age of go, go, go, we sometimes push ourselves so hard that we barely take the time to notice what's going on around us. What things do we value? What holds our interest? What elements work to establish who we are as a group, a nation, a religion, or a race? And who is our favorite Real Housewife?

As you go about life, you shouldn't ignore these important questions, especially if you believe in your right to life, liberty, and pursuit of a good time. While your answers may change, the old saying about the more things change, the more they stay the same rings true, and we see this in the most important parts of everyday life.

Take men's underwear for example. In the 1940s and 1950s, most men wore boxers and their children wore tighty-whities. When the "brief" generation grew up and had kids, their kids wore briefs for a brief time and then started wearing boxers. Now? Who knows?

The attitudes and mindsets of generations can be set or changeable. It's up to us. The following entries are sure to open your mind to just what remarkable creatures we can be . . . when we put our minds to it (and when we're not glued to the DVR).

We Are Experiencing Technical Difficulties

Even though NBC was the first television network to broadcast across America's airwaves in 1941, technically the TV giant is the nation's second network. With the outbreak of World War II, America turned its gaze from entertainment to equipping its armed forces. As a result, it wasn't until after the bombing of Nagasaki at the end of the war in 1945 that companies could file to become official television networks. The first company to do so? The DuMont Television Network. Why? It's a matter of paperwork. DuMont was quicker to apply for and receive its television license after World War II than NBC. It also proved to be the first network to file out of existence. In this case, the late bird definitely got the worm. While the DuMont Television Network became defunct a little more than a decade later, NBC grew into one of the "Big Three" and later "Big Four" networks of modern television. Considered by many today as the "forgotten network," the DuMont Television Network had almost all of its programs destroyed in the 1970s.

Where's Number One

Once upon a time, there was a channel one. In 1945, when the FCC assigned channels, they naturally started at one. But television barged in too quickly on radio's frequency. Its channels hogged up so much of the available bandwidth (a TV channel requires 600 times the bandwidth of a radio channel), the FCC reassigned channel one to be used by people with mobile radios.

Channel ones do exist, just not in the United States.

Close Encounters of the Second Kind:

UFOlogy 101

We've all heard of close encounters of the first kind—a sighting of a UFO within 500 feet. Close encounters of the *second* kind require the sighting of a UFO and some type of physical or electromagnetic action on plants, animals, people, or land. For example, the UFO could be radiating heat or some form of radiation like ultraviolet rays, infrared rays, microwave waves, and/or gamma rays. Any sightings of the consequences of a UFO's radio wave emissions, like scorched land or crop circles from landing or blasting off, could be evidence for an encounter of the second kind—or that it's time to take your medication.

Hynek J. Allen, the father of Ufology, was an astronomy professor at Ohio State and Northwestern University. He founded the Center for UFO Studies in Chicago and devised the Close Encounter System in his book, *The UFO Experience*. Just as you marked your carnal encounters as a teenager, ufologists have seen it fit to categorize their experiences with the unknown in degrees as well. But rather than circling the bases, one's intimacy with aliens is measured in the straightforward closeness of the encounter.

Close Encounters with the Behind

According to the movie, *Close Encounters of the Third Kind*, one must see an alien for an encounter of the third kind. But the only alien encounters people seem to really be concerned about are those that destroy or probe us. Since the Hynek Allen encounter scale only went to the third kind, other Ufologists have added the fourth, fifth, sixth, and even seventh kinds.

The Second-Most-Common Reason to Go Under the Knife:

Which Would You Pick?

The American Society of Plastic Surgeons reports that there were more than 1.5 million plastic or cosmetic surgeries in the United States in 2009, a 9 percent drop from 2008. Even with that drop, more than $10 billion were spent on cosmetic surgery last year. The second-most-common surgery of all? Rhinoplasty. As in nose jobs. About 256,000 nose jobs, or "nose reshapings," as the formerly big-schnozzed prefer to call them, are performed each year. Nose jobs run around $3,500 for the procedure and recovery time is from one to three weeks. For the number one most common plastic surgery, you have to look a little south: breast augmentation. This miracle of science was performed a bra-bursting 289,000 times in 2009.

While it trails in the total number of procedures performed, the nose stands head and shoulders above the breasts when it comes to the diversity of the demographics they serve. For example, while some men who suffer from gyneconmastia (abnormally large mammaries in males) do have their breasts surgically dialed down, their numbers are nowhere near the number of men having their noses prettied up. Men make up nearly 30 percent of all rhinoplasty patients. Also, unlike the leading plastic surgery, rhinoplasty isn't always cosmetic. It can also be performed to correct birth defects or improve breathing problems.

Inflated Numbers

Almost 11 million cosmetic, non-invasive or minimally invasive procedures were performed in 2009. Botox topped the list with 4.8 million procedures, followed by soft tissue fillers (1.7 million), chemical peels (1.1 million), microdermabrasions (910,000), and laser hair removal (893,000). From 2000 to 2009, the number of Botox procedures jumped an incredible 509 percent.

Will The Real American Hero Please Stand Up?

Yo, who? The doll responsible for introducing young boys everywhere to the joys of modern warfare almost wasn't a regular Joe. Rocky the Marine, Ace the Pilot, and Skip the Sailor were the first names suggested for the action figure. And the toy wasn't even the first G.I. Joe. The dude doll, first stationed on store shelves in 1964, took his name from the 1945 movie, *The Story of G.I. Joe.*

At 11½ inches tall, the first G.I. Joe stands roughly six times shorter than the size of the average man. Yet, he stands eye to eye with Barbie. It's only fitting that G.I. Joe would measure up to Barbie, since he probably owes his existence to her. Toy Manufacturers wanted a "doll" boys could play with, but not be called a "doll," thus the birth of the "action figure." Eventually, the 11½-inch version was replaced with an 8-inch version. This second, more mobile soldier had a new feature: a hand that could hold weapons, gear, and anything else Joe might want to grip in order to help him survive long nights in his foxhole. Armed with his "kung fu grip," the second Joe was well on his way to putting the "action" back into action figures.

Battle Wounds

Who gave G.I. Joe the scar on his right cheek? It wasn't Cobra; it was the country he is sworn to defend. Since the U.S. Patent Office would not issue patents for the human figure in general, the makers of G.I. Joe had to give him some sort of distinguishing feature.

The Second Wireless TV Remote Control:

Father of the Couch Potato

In 1956, Robert Adler, the pioneer of the remote control, invented the second wireless remote. Dr. Adler used ultrasound waves in his "Space Command" wireless remote. The remote had four buttons that controlled power, sound, and up-and-down channel select. It had four aluminum rods that gave off different frequencies when the buttons were pressed, sort of like piano keys hitting strings. The remote didn't require batteries, but expensive vacuum tubes were needed in the TV set. Nine million of the Space Commands were produced until infrared remotes were developed in the 1980s. When asked about how his invention created couch potatoes, Dr. Alder said "I don't take responsibility for couch potatoes. They really should exercise."

About a year before Dr. Adler's ultrasound waves hit stores, college dropout and former stock boy for the Zenith Radio Corporation Eugene Polley invented the first wireless TV remote control. His remote was called the "Flashmatic." The Flashmatic depended on four light sensitive photocells located in the four corners of the TV. As an added bonus, bright, sunny days could interfere with its signal, causing it to start changing channels as if possessed. No word on how many people tried to have their remotes exorcised of their demons.

A Lazy Bone for the Lazy Boy
The very first TV remote control turned sixty years old in 2010. It was called the "Lazy Bone" and was invented by the Zenith Radio Corporation. It could turn the TV on *or* off and change channels but it had one major drawback: it wasn't wireless. It had a bulky cable attached to the TV that caused repeated tripping—but it was never lost!

No More Gray People

T he second color TV broadcast signal was developed by RCA and became the national standard on December 17, 1953. As you've probably noticed, it remains to this day. Since NBC was owned by RCA, their shows were the second shows to be broadcast in color. NBC used the RCA system to broadcast the first coast to coast color program, the Tournament of Roses Parade, to twenty-one TV stations.

The first color TV broadcast signal was sent out by CBS in October 1950. Unfortunately, the CBS broadcast signal technology was doomed to fail for three reasons: the poor quality of the system, the commencement of the Korean War, and the resulting production prohibition on color TV sets.

Color TV had a tough go in its early years. One reason was the cost of the sets was more than $1,000 (about $10,000, today). By the mid-1960s, all networks were broadcasting some shows in color and NBC had begun broadcasting all of its shows in color by November 7, 1966. In 1972, the number of color TV sets sold finally outnumbered the black-and-white sets.

Help from a Dummy

The Howdy Doody Show helped NBC gain in popularity during the 1950s. The show starred Buffalo Bob Smith (Robert Schmidt), his freckle-faced marionette sidekick, Howdy Doody, and Clarabell the Clown—a clown that went on to become a kangaroo. Clarabell was played by Bob Keeshan, who later became Captain Kangaroo. *The Howdy Doody Show* was the first show to be broadcast in color, run five days a week, and air more than 1,000 continuous episodes. Well that's a fine howdy-do.

The Second-Most-Common Pet:

Here, Kitty, Kitty

A recent National Pet Owners survey found that 62 percent of American households own a pet. This is up from the 1988 survey when only 56 percent of households had a pet. And there is some good news and bad news for dog lovers. According to the American Pet Products Association, dogs are number one in the number of households that have a pet with 45.6 million households. Cats are number two in that category with a total of 38.2 million households. However, dogs rank second in total population of pet mammals at 77.5 million canines, whereas there are 93.6 million felines in the United States. As you may have witnessed by watching *Hoarders*, it seems that many households have more than one cat. Looks like these days, the cat is the top dog.

Studies suggest there are many health benefits of having pets. Walking a dog can help calm a person's nerves. People who suffer from hypertension have reported drops in blood pressure after they've adopted a dog or cat. Pet ownership can also help fight off depression and loneliness and encourage a new interest in life. The National Institutes of Health even found that pet owners make fewer doctor visits concerning non-serious medical conditions. Unfortunately, few advancements have been made in the field of pet hair removal.

Pet Scoop

- Freshwater fish in aquariums are the largest number of any kind of pet with over 171 million. Cats only take second prize in the mammal category. As any kid whose parents bought them a fish growing up knows, you can't really count fish as pets.
- Americans will spend about $47 million on pet food, supplies, vet visits, grooming, boarding, and live animal purchases in 2010.
- More Americans own reptiles (13.6 million) than horses (13.3 million).

Maybe They're **Both** *Alive*

The King of Rock and Roll almost had to share his throne. The Queen Mother, Gladys Love Presley, was expecting twins. When she delivered her first son, Jesse Garon Presley, he was stillborn. Thirty-five minutes later she had her second son, Elvis Aaron Presley. He was an identical twin of the first child. Vernon Elvis Presley and his wife did not have any more children, but did become very closely attached to Elvis. His parents took him to church regularly, and it was in church that he discovered his musical inspiration that would help him become one of the most popular singers of the twentieth century.

Elvis had some notable seconds in his life: His second movie, *Loving You*, was where he got his first screen kiss. His second gospel album, *How Great Thou Art*, won him his first Grammy award. His second Grammy came from another gospel album, *He Touched Me*. In fact, all of Elvis's Grammys are for gospel albums. Elvis is second only to the Beatles in the total number of number one songs with 18. He is also second in overall album sales with 117.5 million to the Beatles 166.5 million.

Elvis Facts

- Elvis, Elvis Presley, and Graceland are all trademarked names of Elvis Presley Enterprises.
- In 2008, Forbes.com reported that the top-earning dead celebrity from 2007 to 2008 was Elvis. It's believed that the thirtieth anniversary of his death caused a surge in visitors to Graceland, earning his dead body $52 million.
- Elvis ranks number one in the number of gold albums with ninety-seven. The number two spot is held by Barbra Streisand with fifty-one.

9 The Second-Highest and Fastest Roller Coaster:

The Second Quickest Way to Lose Your Lunch

It's hard to imagine a coaster higher or faster than the Top Thrill Dragster at Cedar Point in Sandusky, Ohio, which stands almost 420 feet and reaches 120 miles per hour. But Kingda Ka, at Six Flags in Jackson, New Jersey, is 36 feet higher and reaches 8 miles per hour faster, moving the Top Thrill Dragster to second place.

The Top Thrill Dragster is named after a drag racing funny car. The launch site has the red, yellow, and green starting lights like at a real dragster race and its workers even dress like a pit crew. In a mere 4 seconds after takeoff, riders are cruising at 120 miles per hour while hanging on for dear life. The ride races up its 420-foot tower at a 90-degree angle. Then, over the top with a 90-degree descent. As it's coming down, this Thrill does its best to spill its riders' lunches as it whips them through a 270-degree spiral. The ride only lasts thirty seconds but, as one reviewer noted, "The Top Trill Dragster gives one a dragon-slaying sense of accomplishment onto riders that few coasters can match."

Quick Coaster Facts

- The Steel Dragon 2000 at Nagashima Spa Land in Japan is the world's longest coaster, with 8,133 feet of track.
- If the Incredible Hulk roller coaster didn't have its own power generator, a brownout would occur in Orlando every time it took off.
- Cedar Point has more coasters than any other park with seventeen, followed by Six Flags Magic Mountain's fifteen.

We Have Nothing to Fear (Except for a Couple of Things)

Humans are born with two innate fears: the fear of falling and the fear of sudden, loud noises. For better or worse, as we age, we tend to add additional fears to our list of phobias. A National Institutes of Mental Health report states that about 10 percent of adults have some kind of phobia.

The second-most-common phobia is ophidiophobia, the fear of snakes. Ophidiophobia is one of the most debilitating fears in humans; even the picture of a snake in a magazine or image of one on TV can invoke intense fear in some people. Most people with ophidiophobia live normal lives because they are seldom confronted with a snake. However, when a snake appears, the fear response can be so intense, its reactions can be severe, leading up to and including heart attacks and death. The levels of anxiety can get even stronger when the snake appears to be moving in the direction of the person. The most common learned fear in humans is arachnophobia, the fear of spiders.

Yes, Virginia, You Should Fear Me

Who can't remember their last trip to the circus? If you've shoved it out of your memory, then maybe you suffer from coulrophobia: the fear of clowns. If so, don't worry, you aren't alone. It's estimated 10 percent of people in the United States believe that dressing up as a clown is more appropriate for serial killers than for the celebration of special occasions. For some, their coulrophobia can be so strong that even Santa Claus can cause them to clam up in terror.

Tea for Two

Thirsty for knowledge? Tea is the second-most-commonly drunk beverage in the world. Why not coffee? For starters, tea is much cheaper than coffee. At a market, one may discover six kinds of teas: black, white, green, yellow, oolong, and *pu-erh*. All six varieties come from the same plant, Camillia sinensis. What establishes the differences between the varieties are the different times they are picked and processed. White tea is the youngest and goes through the least amount of processing; the leaves are just steamed and dried. Black tea takes the title as the most processed tea. There are over 3,000 variations of the four basic tea types.

Just as the location of vineyards can affect the wine that grapes transform into, so can the location of tea plants affect the tea's flavor. There is even an olive leaf tea that is gaining popularity. The tea plant belongs to the evergreen family and, if left to grow in the wild, is capable of reaching 30 feet high and living as long as fifty years. A tea picker would need a tall ladder to pick tea from it; currently, a seasoned tea picker can gather 70 pounds of tea a day—that's 14,000 cups of tea!

No surprise here: the gold medal for the most common beverage goes to water.

Anyone else need a pee break?

- Iced tea was first made in America.
- One result of the Boston Tea Party was that Americans started drinking more coffee than tea.
- Tea is good for your skin, bones, teeth, cholesterol level, and blood pressure, and it contains many antioxidants.
- India produces more tea than any other country, followed by Kenya and China.

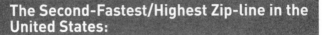

12 The Second-Fastest/Highest Zip-line in the United States:

Zippity Do Da

Z ip-lines are popping up everywhere nowadays. They're taking over theme parks, national parks, and even zoos.

There seems to be a tie for the second-fastest zip-line in the lower forty-eight states between Xtreme Zip in Utah Olympic Park, Utah, and the Heavenly Flyer located on Heavenly Mountain near South Tahoe, California. Both zip riders along at 50 miles per hour. The Xtreme Zip travels above a ski jump, giving the rider a sense of the speed a ski jumper feels as he or she goes down the ski slope. The Utah zip-line holds the record for the world's steepest zip-line, which is perhaps a greater thrill than the speed itself. The Heavenly Flyer, on the other hand, has the longest ride in the lower forty-eight states with a distance of 3,100 feet and an incredible vertical drop of 525 feet.

The longest zip-line in the United States is found in Strait Point, Alaska, with a distance of 5,600 feet, a drop of 1,300 feet, and a top speed close to 60 mph.

You Have Got to Be Crazy
The world's fastest zip-line is found in Sun City, South Africa. On it, you'll hit 87 to 100 miles per hour depending on your weight and body shape. Along the way, you'll drop 919 feet and zip 1.2 miles. The oldest person to ride this zip-line was an eighty-four-year-old Scottish woman. What a brave old fart!

The Second-Longest-Running TV Show:

For Today, Anyway

Television shows come and go, but the one to come without ever going is NBC's *Meet the Press*. The news program began on November 6, 1947, and has racked up more than 4,800 programs. Coming in second is NBC's *Today Show*, which has been on the air since January 14, 1952, and leads all other TV shows with 20,700 plus telecasts.

Sylvester "Pat" Weaver was the vice president at NBC who created the *Today Show*. Not satisfied with merely revolutionizing morning television, Weaver was also responsible for the creation of the *Tonight Show*. The preproduction name of the *Today Show* was *The Rise and Shine Revue*. It began as a two-hour weekday program, but in 1987, it added a one-hour Sunday show. In 1992, the two-hour *Saturday Today* was launched. The weekday show expanded to three hours in 2000 and has been a four-hour show since 2007.

If you want to get technical, the CBS Evening News has been around longer than the *Today Show*, but it's a newscast, not a TV show.

A Memorable Mugg

One of the most memorial gimmicks of the early *Today Show* was J. Fred Muggs, a chimpanzee who served as the show's mascot from 1953 to 1957. A former *Today* producer once estimated that the popularity of Muggs generated about $100 million for NBC. Regrettably, J. Fred Muggs was given his banana slip from the show after he allegedly bit actress Martha Raye on the elbow. Muggs was replaced with a less hungry chimpanzee, Kokomo, but by 1958, the *Today Show* had become a chimp-free zone.

The Second All-Talking Feature Motion Picture:

The End of Silence

It's a wonder that anyone used to go to the movies at all. The first motion pictures were in black and white and had no sound. The technology for putting a soundtrack on film took longer to perfect than the art of capturing an image so filmmakers decided to go the half-assed method: a movie where only some parts had sound. The first motion picture with a partial soundtrack was *The Jazz Singer*, released in 1927. Once they figured out the technology, the second all-talking movie was *On with the Show*, released in 1929. While it might have been only the second talking movie, it was the first talking *color* full-length motion picture. But just barely; Warner Brothers had released another color film, *The Desert Song*, earlier, but it was in both color and black and white. The worldwide gross receipts for *On with the Show* were nearly $2,000,000. Hollywood began seeing the opportunity in making color motion pictures and, after 1929, did just that. Regrettably, the original Technicolor negative of *On with the Show* has been lost and only the black-and-white version survives.

The first all-talking motion picture was *The Lights of New York*, released by Warner Brothers in 1928. The production cost of *The Lights of New York* was $28,000, but it wound up grossing over $1,000,000.

You Ain't Heard Nothing Yet

George Jessel, star of the original *The Jazz Singer*, was asked to star in a film version, but he turned it down. Al Jolson became the second person to take on the role of Jackie Rabinowitz. While Jessel's career leveled off as a Hollywood toastmaster, Jolson's star kept shooting. You may not know it today, but Al Jolson was considered the greatest entertainer in the first half of the twentieth century.

Waters's World

If you've seen *Gone with the Wind*, you undoubtedly remember Hattie McDaniel as Mammy. Not only did she win the 1939 Academy Award for Best Supporting Actress, she was also the first African American *and* African-American woman to win an Academy Award. Pioneers may blaze the trails, but it takes followers to maintain them.

And Ethel Waters was no ordinary follower. Considered to be the first black superstar, Waters gained solo star standing in the mostly white world of vaudeville, radio, film, television, and Broadway on her way to becoming the second African-American woman to take home an Academy Award. Ethel made her film debut in 1929 in one of the first talking motion pictures, *On with the Show*. She was also the first African American to appear on network television in the NBC's variety special, *The Ethel Waters Show* in 1939. But it was her role as "Pinky's Granny" (seriously, that's how she was cast) in 1949's Pinky that would earn her statue and secure her place in seconds history.

No One Puts Ethel Waters in the Corner

- Her recordings of "Am I Blue," "Stormy Weather," and "Dinah" received the Grammy Hall of Fame Award.
- In 2004, Ethel's rendition of "Stormy Weather" became one of twenty recordings selected to be placed in the National Recording Registry in the Library of Congress.
- Ethel Waters was honored by the U.S. Postal Service with a commemorative stamp in 1994.

---

a Nutty Case

The second-most-popular tree nut is a true American, the pecan. The pecan is one of the few commercially grown nuts native to the United States. Almond Joy is not just a candy bar—it must be how Americans feel about the almond, because it's the most popular tree nut in the United States.

Number two isn't the pecan's only numerical claim to fame. Pecan trees can grow to tremendous heights, with most ranging from 70 to 100 feet and some even reaching 150 feet or higher. The per capita consumption of pecans in the United States is 0.48 pounds a year. And while Georgia is more commonly known for its peaches, it is also the top producer of pecans (88 million pounds per year), followed by Texas and New Mexico. At one time, America exported pecans but now, because of higher U.S. demand, America now imports pecans from Mexico. Still, the United States grows 80 percent of all the pecans in the world. However, Mexican pecans are in high demand because their low-humidity climate produces a pecan with a higher ratio of kernel to shell.

Nutritiously Nutty Pecans

- Pecans are full of nineteen vitamins and minerals, including vitamin A, several B vitamins, vitamin E, folic acid, calcium, magnesium phosphorus, potassium, and zinc.
- Pecans rank number 14 on webmd.com's list of top antioxidant rich foods. Pecans contain the antioxidants, vitamin E, ellagic acid, and flavonoids, which help prevent oxidation in cells that can lead to diseases.
- Pecans can lower cholesterol, are heart healthy, and can help in weight control.

E very twenty-six seconds, a car is stolen in America. Most of these cars are never found, they are stripped for parts or smuggled out of the country. In 2009, the second-most-common target for car thieves was the 1995 Honda Civic. The most common target? The 1994 Honda Accord. This raises the question, Why steal a fifteen- or sixteen-year-old car?

There are a few reasons Hondas are so hot. For one, Honda made large numbers of those models. The cars are stripped for parts and are easy to remove and easy to fence. Another reason is that the body styles have changed little from year to year, so one could easily match a part from a 1995 Honda to a 1996 or later model. Also, older Honda vehicles didn't have the more advanced theft-deterrent systems that the newer models have now.

Have even criminals gone green? The 1995 Honda Civic VX was able to get the same mileage as today's hybrids. The Civic VX Hatchback, with its I-4 1.5 liter 92 horsepower gasoline engine and five-speed transmission, turned in an EPA city mileage of forty-seven miles per gallon and highway fifty-six miles per gallon. Please bring this car back!

Please Steal This Car
The top ten least stolen vehicles: Mercedes E Class, Buick Rainier, Subaru Forester, Buick Terraza, VW New Beetle, Ford Focus, Volvo V70, Toyota Prius, Saturn Relay, and the Ford Freestyle. The car with the highest thief claim frequency in 2007 was the Cadillac Escalade ESV with 15 per 1,000 stolen each year. The wheels and tires on the Escalade can be worth $10,000 alone.

18 The Second-Tallest Wooden Roller Coaster in the United States:

A Wooden Wonder

At a staggering 183 feet, El Toro, located at Six Flags in Jackson, New Jersey, is the United States' second-tallest wooden roller coaster. Wouldn't you know it—with a height of 218 feet, the tallest wooden roller coaster in the United States is the Son of Beast at Kings Island in Cincinnati, Ohio. That's the height of a twenty-story building! Either way, they're both too tall for us.

While second in height, El Toro claims the title of the steepest descent of any wooden roller coaster with its 76-degree angle plunge. The first drop of El Toro is 176 feet, which places it at a stomach-dropping second longest for a wooden coaster in the United States and third in the world. At the bottom of the drop, the El Toro is zipping along at 70 mph—second fastest in the United States.

El Toro is an engineering masterpiece because of its super-smooth ride. Unlike other wooden coasters that are cut, laid down, and nailed by hand, the El Toro track was prefabricated, using lasers to cut each piece with extreme precision. After they were cut, the pieces of track snapped right together like Lego pieces. This precision in its construction makes the El Toro track as smooth as steel coaster tracks.

Coal Coaster
The first roller coaster in the United States was a converted coal train in the Pennsylvanian mountains called Mauch Chunk Switchback Railroad. When the train stopped hauling coal, people jumped in its cars for a ride down the tracks. The oldest operating roller coaster in the United States is the Leap the Dips in Lakemont, Pennsylvania. It's been operating since 1902 and is a National Landmark.

19 The Second-Largest Ice Cream-Loving City:

We All Scream for Seconds!

Americans love their ice cream so much that they're the highest per capita consumers of the creamy treat in the world. Annually, U.S. consumption is estimated at 23.2 quarts of ice cream, ice milk, sherbet, and other frozen dairy treats per person. So what American city is second-to-one in their love for ice cream? That would be St. Louis, Missouri.

Crown Candy Kitchen in St. Louis is one of the oldest and most popular attractions in the city. Crown Candy features the 1904 World's Fair sundae with 14 percent butterfat ice cream. Since 1913, the Kitchen has issued an ice cream challenge: drink five shakes in thirty minutes and the shakes are free, your name is immortalized on a plaque, and your bowels will never be the same.

Another famous St. Louis ice cream spot, Route 66 survivor Ted Drewes, doesn't even serve ice cream. Instead, it scoops out concretes, cones, and sundaes of frozen custard. Frozen custard is made like ice cream, but with the addition of eggs. Ted Drewes makes his iconic concrete so thick that servers turn the concrete upside down before handing it to the customer without any of its goodness spilling out.

If all this info hasn't yet given you a brain-freeze, here's the scoop on number one: Portland, Oregon, takes the blue ribbon for ice cream consumption.

The First Ice Cream Cornucopia
During the 1904 World's Fair in St. Louis, Earnest Hamwi was selling cups of ice cream when he ran out of dishes. The resourceful Hamwi asked a nearby waffle vendor if he would roll his waffles into the shape of a "cornucopia" so he could put his ice cream in it and, behold: the World's Fair Cornucopia. The name was later changed to the less corny "ice cream cone."

The Second-Leading Banana Consumers:

Second Banana

There's no doubt that for Americans, bananas have a real appeal. The United States consumes 26 percent of all exported bananas, coming in a distant second to Europe, which consumes a staggering 39 percent.

According to the latest numbers on worldwide exports, 80 million tons of bananas are exported every year. That comes out to about 30 pounds of bananas for every person on the planet. But that'll barely last a month for someone living in Uganda. Ugandans eat about 1⅓ pounds of bananas a day. Amazingly, around 130 countries in the world produce bananas, even though 60 percent of the world's production comes from India with 21 percent followed by China, the Philippines, Brazil, and Ecuador, each with about 9 percent of the crop. The largest exporters of bananas are Ecuador, Costa Rica, the Philippines, and Columbia with 64 percent of the world's exports. Ecuador leads all the other countries with 30 percent of the global exports of bananas. Recently, there has been an increase in the amount of organic and fair trade bananas produced in the world. The Dominican Republic leads the world in the production of organic bananas. The Dominican Republic, Ecuador, Peru, Ghana, Columbia, and the Windward Islands are all leading exporters of free-trade bananas.

An All-Purpose Plant
The banana fruit isn't the only part of the plant people use: banana leaves serve several second purposes since they are large, flexible, and waterproof. Food can be wrapped in banana leaves when cooking to enhance its taste and aroma. The colorful leaves can also be used to make eco-friendly plates.

The Second-Greatest Potato-Consuming Region of the World:

One Potato, Two Potato . . .

The world's second-biggest fans of potatoes? That titles goes to the North Americans (in the United States and Canada), who average 132 pounds per capita in one year. Europeans, especially the Russians, eat more potatoes per capita than any other major region of the world, with a total of 194 pounds. That is a little more than a half a pound of potatoes a day. The country with the highest per capita potato consumption is Uganda, at 1,050 pounds a year, or more than three pounds a day.

Would you guess that China is the world's largest producer of potatoes? It is, but because its population is so high, its per capita potato consumption is only about 40 pounds a year.

Today, almost every state in the Union grows potatoes, with the largest producing states being Idaho, Washington, Wisconsin, North Dakota, and Colorado. Americans like their processed potatoes: French fries, potato chips, and dehydrated potatoes account for 60 percent of potato production. Fresh potato consumption is only a third of the U.S. potato crop. Potatoes were first grown by settlers in Canada during the mid-1600s; now potatoes are Canada's most valuable horticultural crop. What do Canadians do with so many potatoes? They're the largest exporter of frozen French fries in the world.

Potato Facts

- Scientists believe that the first potatoes were cultivated around 8,000 years ago near Lake Titicaca, between Peru and Bolivia in the Andes Mountains.
- There are 4,300 different kinds of potatoes grown in the Andes.
- The first potato chip is thought to have been invented by chef George Crum at Saratoga Springs, New York, in 1853.

The Second-Largest User of Locally Grown Produce:

Can We Get a Second, Por Favor?

When it comes to relying upon locally grown food, Chipotle Mexican Grill stands alone in its commitment. Currently, no other restaurant chain on the planet has a similar commitment anywhere close to what Chipotle is doing in their mission to "Serve Food with Integrity." Nearly everything from the onions and oregano that spice the sauces to the peppers that provide the heat comes from local, family-owned farms. In fact, the produce used at one-third of all Chipotles travels less than 50 miles to get in your belly. That may not sound like much, until you consider that on average, produce in American restaurants travels 1,500 miles from plot to plate. And gas isn't the only toxic chemical Chipotle helps to reduce. The burrito bar's use of organically grown beans alone is directly responsible for the reduction of 100,000 pounds of pesticides since 2005. In 2010, Chipotle even raised its commitment by stating half of all produce used in its restaurants will come from local farms. That translates into 5 million pounds of produce bought from local farmers.

So, number two, where are you?

Bur·ri·to: A Tasty Treat; A Small Donkey

To most Americans, a burrito is a tortilla wrapped around as much beans, meat, cheese, and whatever else fits. Translated, though, burrito is nothing more than a tiny donkey. What's the connection? No one knows for certain, but most explanations—just like a good night in Tijuana—involve a donkey. Since donkeys were the first food trucks for miners and other laborers, the burrito's name was most likely inspired by its method of delivery.

23   The Second-Beefiest State in the United States:

Where's the Beef?

W hile number one is no surprise, you might find it surprising that Missouri has the second-highest number of beef cattle. Numero uno? Texas, of course.

Several states, Kansas, Nebraska, California, and Oklahoma, have more *cattle* than Missouri, but not all of those cows are for dinner; many of them are dairy cows. Missouri has more than 60,000 beef cattle producers and more than 2.161 million beef cattle. Most of the state's beef farms and ranches are located in the southwest corner of the state. Texas has a human population of about 24 million and a cattle population of over 13.8 million heads of all kinds of cattle (eatin' and drinkin').

Beef cattle production is the largest part of American agriculture. More than 31 percent of all American farms are classified as beef cattle operations and 97 percent of those operations are family farms as opposed to being large, corporate farms. U.S. beef consumption in 2008 was 59.9 pounds per capita, with chicken as a close second at 59.2 pounds per capita.

Unbelievable Beef Facts

- The American version of the hamburger is more than 100 years old, making its debut at the 1904 St. Louis World's Fair.
- White Castle was America's first hamburger chain.
- The longhorn cow was the first breed introduced into the United States.
- There are more cattle than people in nine states: Idaho, Iowa, Kansas, South Dakota, North Dakota, Wyoming, Nebraska, Montana, and Oklahoma.

The Second Reality TV Show:

Surviving the Real World

It might be hard to tell, but there was a time when American viewers craved fiction from their sets. America's version of *Survivor* was the second reality show to buck the trend when it became the second reality show to air in America in 2000.

That first show to start the reality show onslaught occurred in 1992, when MTV launched the first reality series, *The Real World*.

Eight years later, CBS transported the "reality" MTV had created from the loft apartments of America's hippest neighborhoods to some of the most extreme habitats on the planet with their *Survivor* franchise. About three years prior, *Expedition Robinson* debuted in Sweden. Even though the American version is based on this Swedish version, several significant changes were made. The most glaring: the American version has only sixteen castaways competing for a million dollar prize, as opposed to forty-eight contestants trying to survive for the $33,000 jackpot. Neither show was without controversy. The first *Survivor* winner, Richard Hatch, found himself surviving a federal penitentiary for not paying proper taxes on his winnings. In Sweden, a contestant on *Expedition Robinson* jumped in front of a train out of shame for having been the first voted off.

Keep on Surviving

The second person to win *Survivor* was better at firsts than seconds. Tina Wesson was the first woman to win the game. She was also the first winner not to be convicted of a felony. Most impressively, though, she was the first (and only) contestant to make it through a game without receiving a single vote during tribal council. But when she had a second chance to win the game in the first all-star edition of the program, she was the first person voted off.

25 The Second-Greatest Producer of Tomatoes:

The Fruit Brought Before the U.S. Supreme Court

Americans sure do love their tomatoes—we are the second-largest producer of fresh market tomatoes in the world. Since China has the world's largest human population, it should be no surprise that it's also the world's largest producer of tomatoes. The United States has a human population of only a quarter as many people! That's a lot of tomatoes per capita. The two top tomato-growing states are Florida (with about 1,455 million pounds produced annually) and California (supplying approximately 1,230 million pounds a year). All the rest of the states combined grow around 1,017 million pounds each year.

The tomato made history by being the first fruit or vegetable to make it all the way to the U.S. Supreme Court in 1893. At the time, there was a 10 percent duty on imported vegetables, but fruits had no duty. It was ruled by the court that the tomato was a vegetable and not a fruit. Botanically speaking, the tomato *is* a fruit because it has seeds inside it. In fact, the tomato is the world's most popular fruit. The first Spanish explorers found that the Aztecs and Incas were growing tomatoes on their conquest of Mexico and South America. The Spaniards took the tomato plants to their other colonies and back to Europe.

A Tomato Tree?
In an experimental greenhouse in Disney's tech-themed park, Epcot, you'll find the only single-vine tomato plant in the United States. It produces thousands of golf ball-sized tomatoes annually, some of which are even served at the Walt Disney World Resort's eating establishments.

The Second-Greatest—Per-Capita Turkey-Eating Country:

Gobble Gobble

Well, this seems to be a no-brainer for most people. Of course, the United States is the top turkey consumer in the world—wrong! That distinction goes to Israel, where the average per capita turkey gobbling is 22 pounds. Most Israelis slow roast their turkeys on a spit at a Shawarma stand. Also popular is the turkey schnitzel. The United States comes in second with a per capita turkey consumption of 17 pounds. U.S. turkey consumption has doubled since 1970 with more turkey being eaten during the year, not just on holidays. In 1970, around 50 percent of all turkey consumption took place around the holidays; now holiday turkey consumption makes up only about 29 percent. It's estimated that 45 million turkeys are eaten on Thanksgiving, 22 million on Christmas, and 19 million on Easter. About 95 percent of Americans claim to eat turkey on Thanksgiving. Turkey breast meat is one of the best sources of protein, and it has virtually no saturated fat. More good nutritional news: no steroids or growth hormones are given to any turkeys consumed in the United States. Minnesota leads the country in the number of turkeys raised with 48 million followed by North Carolina with a total of 40 million.

Turkey Talk

- Wild turkeys can run 20 mph and fly 55 mph for short distances. Domesticated turkeys cannot fly.
- The first meal on the moon eaten by Neil Armstrong and Buzz Aldrin was foil-packed, roasted turkey.
- The Pilgrims and early settlers were familiar with how to raise turkeys because early explorers brought turkeys back to Europe in the 1500s, where they were raised for food.

The Second Gum:

Dubble Bubble

In 1928, an accountant from the Fleer Chewing Gum Company, Walter Diemer, took a second chomp at creating a chewing gum specially designed to blow bubbles. What he came up with was the pink gum of little league baseball concessions and parade floats everywhere: Dubble Bubble.

Frank Fleer invented the first bubble gum called Blibber-Blubber in 1906. Unfortunately, though, the gum was hard to chew and it didn't hold its flavor well. And if that weren't enough, a popped bubble from this gum was so sticky that it ruined clothes. This first bubble gum was never sold commercially.

While experimenting with different recipes, Diemer botched one, but noticed his "accident" had produced a gum that was less sticky and stretched more easily than any of his previous batches. Selling for a penny a piece, Dubble Bubble made more than $1.5 million in its first year. Amazingly, while Diemer did wind up climbing the corporate ladder at Fleer to the office of senior vice president, he never received a single royalty for his bubblicious second.

Forget the Alamo, Remember the Chicle!

Who would've guessed that Mexican General, Santa Anna, who defeated Davy Crockett at the Alamo, would come to the rescue of future gum chewers? After his capture at the Battle of San Jacinto, he was exiled to the home of inventor Thomas Adams on Staten Island. The general convinced Adams he could make a fortune from a tropical root chewed in Mexico called *chicle*. Adams combined the *chicle* with paraffin wax and chewing gum was well on its way to the bottoms of desks in schools across the nation.

Cool Treat

How old do you have to be to be an inventor? How about eleven years old? The inventor of the Popsicle, Frank Epperson, was an eleven-year-old boy from San Francisco, who accidentally left a cup of powdered soda, water, and a stirring stick outside on a porch on a winter night in 1905. Little did Frank know that the temperature would drop and the next morning he would find a frozen concoction that would become the first Popsicle. Frank tasted it and is said to have shown it to his friends, but did not do anything with his new idea until eighteen years later. Frank called his frozen treat an "Epsicle" when it first debuted in 1923 at an Alameda, California, amusement park.

But Frank's children called the treat a "Pop's-sicle" and convinced their pop to change its name to Popsicle. In 1925, Frank teamed up with the Joe Lowe Company in New York, which distributed the Popsicle around the United States. A mascot, Popsicle Pete, was introduced to help market the treat. Currently, more than two billion Popsicles are sold each year, and there are more than thirty different flavors, of which cherry and orange are the most popular.

Pete's Popsicle Prizes
Popsicle Pete was created and drawn by Woody Gelman, the same artist that drew Bazooka Joe, the bubble gum mascot. Pete was a red-blooded, redheaded, All-American kid. Pete even had a pony, Chiefy, who helped Pete with his promotions. If a kid collected enough Popsicle Pete coupons from inside the Popsicle wrappers, he or she could redeem them for prizes and fillings.

29 The Second-Longest-Running Show on Broadway:

In "Memory" of an Alley Cat

M e-ow. The musical *Cats* is the second-longest-running show on Broadway, boasting 7,485 consecutive performances. Andrew Lloyd Webber's musical featuring grown adults dressed up like felines was taken from T. S. Eliot's book of poems, *Old Possum's Book of Practical Cats*. *Cats* previewed on Broadway at the Winter Garden Theatre on September 23, 1982, and closed on September 10, 2000. This was actually its second opening. The very first performance of *Cats* was in London, at the New London Theatre on May 11, 1981, where it continued for 8,949 performances before closing on its twenty-first birthday in 2002.

Cats has been professionally produced in more than thirty countries around the world and translated into twenty languages. The production of *Cats* won two Oliver Awards for the Best New Musical and Outstanding Achievement of the Year in Musicals in 1981. *Cats* also received seven Tony Awards in 1983, including Best Musical.

On January 9, 2006, Andrew Lloyd Webber's *The Phantom of the Opera* became the longest running show on Broadway. With over 8,500 consecutive performances, since its 1988 opening, it's still pulling in audiences today.

The Many Lives of a Phantom

The Phantom of the Opera has had about as many lives as a cat. Born as a French novel in 1909, it has struggled to stay in print, despite success in other mediums. In 1925, *The Phantom* menaced silver screens across the country as a silent film hit. Then, in 1976, *Phantom* climbed on stage in Ken Hill's well received, but now forgotten, musical. That makes Webber's, the second stage version of this tragic story.

The Second-Bestselling Smartphone in the United States:

Droid Wars

I t sounds like a battle of robots but in fact, we're talking about smartphones, those fancy little cellphones that basically act like the mini computer you always dreamed of having as a kid. The second-bestselling smart phone on the market? The Droid.

BlackBerry has dominated the smartphone market for several years and has the bestselling smartphones going. In 2010, the Motorola Droid leapfrogged the Apple iPhone to capture the position of second-bestselling smartphone in the United States. The Droid has thousands of standard applications a user can choose from, as well as a first: a 5-megapixel camera with dual LED flash. The Droid's 3.7-inch screen is the largest screen on any of the smartphones. This Droid can also surf the web faster and show more of the web than its competitors. It's also the first phone to come with Google Maps navigation, which made the Droid the best GPS phone available.

Simon Says Smartin' Up

About the same time the wristwatch calculator began to go the way of the pocket protector, IBM unleashed the first smartphone unto the world. The IBM Simon first hit hips in 1993 with cutting-edge apps such as a calendar, address book, world clock, and calculator. Priced at just a penny under $900, the phone struggled to find a large market.

The Second Use of a Limestone Mine:
Some Mighty Mine Mushrooms

What happens to a mined-out mine? Since mines provide an ideal environment for mushrooms to grow, Creekside Mushrooms Ltd. in Worthington, Pennsylvania, has seized the opportunity to get a second use out of an exhausted mine. Its mine is 300 feet underground and has about 150 miles of tunnels. The mushroom company can grow mushrooms year-round because growers can easily monitor and maintain perfect growing conditions. Each day, some mushrooms are being harvested and new ones are being started, thus providing an uninterrupted supply of fresh mushrooms all year long. Creekside Mushrooms is the only underground mushroom farm in the United States, and it's the largest mushroom-growing facility in the world.

While these mushrooms may not be magically tremendous, they are magically nutritious. They're fat-free, sodium-free, and low in calories. They're also rich in riboflavin, fiber, niacin, vitamin B5, and copper. Perhaps the most amazing nutritional fact about mushrooms is that unlike fruits and vegetables, this fungi has vitamin D. Mushroom growers even have the capacity to increase the amount of vitamin D in their mushrooms by exposing them to ultraviolet light. Just as in humans, exposure to ultraviolet light can produce vitamin D in mushrooms.

The Circle of Seconds

Mushrooms aren't the only seconds in mines. Even before they were converted to harvest mushrooms, mines were home to stores of organic material waiting for their second shot at the Earth's surface. Coal started out as some sort of dead plant (scientists believe a fern-like species) material. Then, over the course of millions of years, it fossilized into the fuel of electric generators across the globe.

Still Rushin'

The United States not only finished second to China in overall medals and gold medal totals for the 2008 Olympic Games, it also ranks second in global gold production. Even without its record haul of fifty-one gold medals in the 2008 Beijing Olympic Games, China would still lead the world in gold production.

The United States only recently surpassed long-time second, South Africa, in gold production. Most of the United States' gold is found in Alaska and Nevada, with the largest mines found in northern Nevada. Only about thirty mines account for most of the gold production in the United States. There are two primary places to look for gold deposits. A lode, or vein, deposit is where gold is located in veins and cracks in rocks. The other type of deposit, a placer deposit, occurs when water erosion on the of veins causes gold particles to settle on the bottom of streams.

Gold has some very remarkable features. It's very soft and the most malleable and ductile of all the elements. Gold can be hammered so thin that you can see through it. In fact, one ounce of gold could be drawn into a thin wire 50 miles long! Best of all, one type of radioactive gold isotope, Au 198, with a half-life of 2.7 days, is used in the treatment of several types of cancer.

Olympic Gold

Ever wonder why so many of the gold products you buy are only "gold-plated" rather than solid gold? Because if every gold product were solid gold, there wouldn't be any left. Believe it or not, all the gold ever mined would fit into just two Olympic-sized swimming pools.

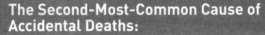

A Dangerous Mix

This one might surprise you (and cause you to think twice before you fill your next prescription). The second-leading cause of accidental deaths in the United States, taking 27,532 lives, is accidental drug poisoning. It's probably *no* surprise that automobile accidents are the leading cause of accidental deaths (43,664 lives) in the United States. But, the number of auto deaths has been going down for the last decade.

The Centers for Disease Control (CDC) has reported that between 1999 and 2004, there has been a 68 percent increase in poisonings due to accidental, yet deadly drug interactions. Doctors are writing more prescriptions for oxycodone, hydrocodone, methadone fentanyl, and other painkillers, and deaths related to these drugs are increasing. According to *Science Daily*, "between 1999 and 2002, the number of overdose death certificates mentioning poisoning by opioid pain killers went up by 91 percent." While these drugs might have a purpose, they can kill more than just pain if mixed with the wrong medications. It should be pointed out that many of the over-the-counter medicines on the shelf today were prescription drugs just a few years ago.

Online Assistance

Online "drug interaction checkers"—available on websites of major medical centers, retailers, and pharmacies such as Caremark, the University of Maryland Medical Center, Drugs.com, Eckerd, Discovery Health, Drugstore.com, and Express Scripts—allow patients to plug in the names of their medications and produce a report that lists their possible interactions with certain foods, alcohol, and other drugs.

---

34 The Second-Most-Popular Candy in the United States:

It Took a War to Create a Candy

The two most popular candies in America aren't candy bars. They're candy pieces. The second-most-popular candy is M&M's, and at the top is Reese's Pieces. The idea for M&M's was developed during the Spanish Civil War when Forrest Mars saw soldiers eating chocolate covered with a hard sugar coating. The sugar coating kept the chocolate from melting in the hot Spanish sun. The major problem chocolate makers always had was that their products would always melt in the summer. So, summer chocolate sales always dropped off. Mars patented the process for coating chocolate with a hard candy shell in 1941. Since the M&M candies did not melt in the summer, it was a win-win for the consumer and candy maker. M&M's were given to American soldiers as treats during the World War II. The famous M was imprinted in black on the candies for the first time in 1950. Today, the imprinting machine can etch 2.6 million M&M's an hour and 100,000,000 M&M's a day.

The Second M in M&M's

The second M in the M&M brand stands for Murrie—Bruce Murrie to be exact. Bruce's dad, William Murrie, had run the Hershey Chocolate Company for many years, and candy maker Forrest Mars wanted Hershey to supply the chocolate for his candy coated chocolates. He even offered to call them M&M's for Mars and Murrie. Bruce became Forrest's partner, and M&M's were born.

Blazing Bike Shorts

Does biking make you young and smart, or do young, smart people just tend to bike? Regardless of the answer, Portland, Oregon, is more than just a "youth magnet"—it's also the second-most-bike-friendly city in the world. As growth in many cities across the country contracts, their youth are among the first to go once the jobs dry up. So, what's a kid to do? Move to Portland. Not only is the cost of living lower than it is in most major cities, but you can also save money on gas by riding your bike to work. Almost one out of ten Portlanders pedal to work, and the city continues to make improvements for bikers' ease and safety. Only Minneapolis ranks higher.

Bicycles aren't the only things that place Portland second. She claims seconds to coffee and statues, too. Only Seattle has more coffeeshops per capita in the United States. And, as far as statues of hand-pounded copper go, Portland's Portalandia is second to one: the Statue of Liberty. But you'll have to go to Portland to see her because she won't be placed on any t-shirts or coffee mugs anytime soon. Her creator, Raymond Kaskey, was careful to secure all of the rights to her image.

Cycling Through the Tulips

Virtually every list compiled lists Amsterdam as the universe's "Most Bike-Friendly City." According to online travel guide Trip Advisor, the number two "Thing to Do" in Amsterdam is to take a ride with Mike's Bike Tours. What better way to interact with a city where bicycles make up 40 percent of the traffic?

The Second-Highest-Earning Dead Celebrity:

Good Grief

When it comes to dead celebrity earning power, names like John Lennon, Biggie Smalls, Frank Sinatra, or Tupac Shakur probably come first to mind. But in order to get to the number two celebrity death-earner, you've got to go old school—all the way back to your Sunday morning comic strips. None other than Charles Schulz, the creator of *Peanuts* comic strip, comes in second in terms of earning from beyond the grave. Since embarking on his own, personal journey to see if even cartoon dogs go to heaven in 2000, Schulz has garnered $33 million from his *Peanuts* comics that continue running in daily newspapers. Most of the Charles Schulz estate earnings don't come from the newspapers that still carry his cartoons but from the licensing of his famous characters like Snoopy and Charlie Brown.

Rock-and-roll legend Elvis Presley earned $52,000,000 in 2007–2008 making him the highest-earning celebrity not alive.

No Small Peanuts

Schulz's big break came when the United Feature Syndicate published his first comic strip, titled *Lil' Folks*. The name was changed to *Peanuts* (which supposedly, Schulz never particularly liked) and the comic eventually appeared in more than 2,600 newspapers around the world. The comic strip was made into animated TV specials like *A Charlie Brown Christmas* and *You're a Good Man, Charlie Brown*. Schulz produced his final comic on January 3, 2000, and died just forty days later.

The Second-Most-Caffeinated Country in the World:

Coffee Kingdom

With a Starbucks on every corner, it'd be easy to assume that Americans drink more coffee per capita than any other country. However, Americans don't even rank in the top ten. Norwegians are second highest on the coffee drinking list with an annual consumption of 1,260 cups, or 3.5 cups a day. Why do Norwegians drink so much coffee? It must be to get that lingering lutefisk taste out of their mouths.

Actually, when coffee was first brought to Norway in the 1600s, it was very rare and expensive. However, by 1840, the price became more reasonable because tropical countries like Brazil and Java were producing larger quantities. Unlike most of Europe, where people would go to coffeehouses, Norwegians tended to serve coffee in their homes. Surrounded by brutal cold and darkness for long periods of the year, Norwegians were growing concerned about the increased use of alcoholic beverages. Coffee provided them with somewhat of a suitable alternative. For number one, you only need to head next door to Finland, where the average Finn drinks more than 1,500 cups of coffee a year—about four cups a day.

Columbian Supreme
You may not be able to tell just by drinking it, but coffee is actually a bean. How many other beans have you washed down your bacon with? Coffee is grown in over seventy countries around the world, but the title of the second leading coffee exporter goes to Columbia. And there's a good chance coffee ranks number two on Columbia's own list of exported goods as well.

38 The Second-Most-Expensive House in the World:

Home, Sweet Home

The owner of the second-most-expensive home in the world, Lily Safra, lives in a villa in the city of Villefranche-sur-Mer on the French Riviera. The villa is the $506 million Villa Leopolda, built in 1902 by King Leopold II of Belgium for his mistresses. As it turned out, it was one of many villas he built for his mistresses. Ms. Safra is one of the more respectable habitants, and the widow of the late banker Edmund Safra.

Sitting atop a cliff, the home is rumored to have eleven bedrooms, fourteen bathrooms, a bowling alley, sports courts, a movie theater, and several kitchens and dining rooms. The grounds have swimming pools and prolific gardens set among towering cypress trees that require the attention of more than fifty full-time gardeners. Recently, Mikhail Prokhorov, the second-richest Russian, placed a $53 million down payment on the home but later decided not to buy it. Unfortunately, Mr. Prokhorov must not have read the fine print. A French court later ruled that he could not get his money back.

Owners of the most expensive home in the world, Mukesh and Nita Ambani live in a $1 billion, 27-story, 40,000-square-foot tower called Antilla in Mumbai, India.

I Want to Suck Your Cash
Count Dracula's castle is for sale and it can be had for a horrific $135 million. The castle has fifty-seven rooms and comes furnished with Old World furniture. It does have its downsides: there's no central heat and thousands of tourists still visit the castle even though it's no longer open to visitors. One way to solve the tourist problem might be to let them stay the night.

The Second-Most-Fast-Food Sales:

Forget Plastics—Franchise

Talk about an ambitious high school graduate. Number two in fast-food sales goes to Subway with $9,600,000,000 in yearly receipts. Subway's story started in Bridgeport, Connecticut, in 1965 when recent high school graduate Fred Deluca and family friend Dr. Peter Buck were talking about Fred's future. The good doctor suggested that Fred open a submarine shop and gave him $1,000 to get him started. The two set goals, worked hard, and by 1974, they had sixteen stores throughout Connecticut. Next, they decided to sell franchises of their business as a way to increase its number of restaurants. Their franchise plan worked, and now Subway has more stores in the United States, Canada, and Australia than even McDonalds. Part of Subway's success has been through branching outside the United States. Subways are found in ninety-two countries, and there are 32,945 Subway restaurants in all. In a recent Zagat's Fast-Food Survey, respondents ranked Subway number one-in overall provider of "Healthy Options," "Best Service," and "Most Popular." Subway was also ranked as the number one franchise by *Entrepreneur* magazine in 2010.

Can a fifty-two-year-old man start a business that generates more than $30,025,000,000 annually and be number one in fast-food sales? That's exactly what Ray Kroc, founder of first place McDonald's, did.

Putting the Cow Back in Moscow

The third-largest fast-food restaurant is Burger King, with 12,000 restaurants across all fifty states and in seventy-four countries. In January 2010, Burger King opened its first restaurant in Russia. It's found in northwest Moscow and will soon be followed by one in downtown Moscow.

The Second-Richest Man in America:

Battle of the Nerds

No, it's not Donald Trump. The second-richest man in America is Warren Buffet, the self-made billionaire, who made his money through savvy investing. Buffet's net-worth is estimated at $47 billion—give or take a few billion depending on whether the market is behaving like a bull or a bear.

Buffet had to settle for second place in 2009 after losing $25 billion in the recent stock market downturn. He got his start at thirteen by delivering newspapers; he filled out his first tax return that same year, claiming a $35 deduction for his bicycle. In 1965, Buffet took over the textile firm, Berkshire Hathaway. Buffet's collection of investments is diverse: he is invested in food (Dairy Queen), utilities (MidAmerican Energy), jewelry (Borsheim's), and insurance (Geico). Buffet did hold the distinction of being the richest man in the world in March 2008, when he reached $62 billion.

The richest man in America is Bill Gates, with an estimated $53 billion, depending on how much he is donating to his charitable Gates Foundation.

Moving North of the Number Three Ranking

The third-richest man in the world in 2008 was Carlos Slim Helu, but the latest reports from 2010 suggest that he might be making a move to the top of the list. Carlos is a Mexican telecom tycoon who made much of his money when Mexico decided to privatize its telephone system. His holdings include a mobile phone company, a construction company, an oil-drilling group, newspapers, and a financial group.

Holy Batcrap, That's a Lot of Money

So, where do you stand Batnerds? If forced to choose between the two comics, which would you choose: loyalty to your hero or an extra $600 grand? The *Detective Comics* number 27 swoops in at number two with a price tag of $1,500,000. While Superman is nowhere to be seen, *Detective Comics* number 27 introduces the Dark Knight.

Just like Batman himself, his publisher has gone through several adjustments and reincarnations. *Detective Comic* number 27 was first published in 1939 by National Allied Publications, the same publisher of *Action Comics* number one. National Allied Publications then became *Detective Comics*, which was later shortened to *DC Comics*, now a subsidiary of Time Warner.

The first comic book, *Action Comic* number one, is now worth $2,100,000, making it the most valuable American comic book. And that's not this comic's only first; it was the first comic to feature Superman.

Recession Hero

Comic book collectors have seen prices of extremely rare original copies increase upward between 15 percent and 25 percent during recessions. In 1974, DC Comics published an exact reprint of *Detective Comics* number 27 in its, "Famous First Edition" line that had a stiff outer cover stating it was a reprint. However, if the outer cover is removed, the comic is identical to the original, except for the fact that it's slightly oversized. The story in the *Detective Comics* number 27 was titled "The Case of the Chemical Syndicate," and the script was written by Bill Finger with the pencil and ink drawings believed to be those of comic legend Bob Kane.

And the Oscar Almost Goes to...

While the movie with the second most Oscars doesn't have top bragging rights, at least it is not tied for most wins, as the first is. *West Side Story* boasts a staggering ten Academy Awards to its name. The movie remakes Shakespeare's *Romeo and Juliet* in a setting of New York City's Upper West Side of the 1950s. Rival gangs, instead of families, provide the conflict in the movie. Many critics believe that the movie is the best film adaptation of any musical ever made. *West Side Story* is also considered to be the best musical film produced in the 1960s. The film industry was experiencing incredible competition from TV shows at the time and this movie helped bring people back into the movie theatres again. The albums for *West Side Story*'s Broadway play and movie have both sold over one million copies.

Three motion pictures are tied for having the most Oscars with eleven. They are *Ben-Hur*, *Titanic*, and *The Lord of the Rings: Return of the King*. We'll take second place if it means we get our own statue.

Oscar Trivia

- The two trilogies that have received Best Picture nominations for each of their installments are *The Lord of the Rings* (2001, 2002, and 2003) and *The Godfather* (1972, 1974, and 1990).
- *All About Eve* (1950) and *Titanic* (1997) both received fourteen Oscar nominations—the most for all movies.

Play It Again, but Better This Time

When Arnold Schwarzenegger famously said, "I'll be back," he wasn't kidding. Second place on the list of sequels to out-earn their originals goes to 1991's *Terminator 2: Judgment Day*. Its $204,843,345 in total U.S. gross was a 433.8 percent increase over *The Terminator*'s $38,371,200 in 1984.

The Night of the Living Dead (1990) grossed $5,835,247 in U.S. receipts, while its sequel, *Dawn of the Dead* (2004), did 911.5 percent better by grossing $59,020,957. Most motion picture sequels aren't as good as their originals; they just seem to be cashing in on the success of the first film. *Terminator 2* was the second in the Terminator trilogy but most critics and filmgoers agree that it was the first in overall quality. The movie was directed by James Cameron before he became the "King of the World,"and starred Arnold Schwarzenegger before he became the governor.

Terminator 2 also did pretty well on judgment day, winning four Oscars for Best Sound, Best Makeup, Best Effect–Visual, and Best Effects–Sound Effects Editing. It was also voted the Favorite Motion Picture in the 1992 People's Choice Awards.

Caddy-Stink-Fever

Not all sequels are winners. Actually, most sequels are a distant second compared to their originals. A couple of notable stink-bombs: *Saturday Night Fever* spawned the sequel *Staying Alive* which ranks by many as the number one worst sequel. Coming in a close second is *Caddyshack II* in which the biggest stars from the original—Bill Murray, Rodney Dangerfield, and Ted Knight—aren't even in it.

The Second-Best Place for Artists:

Not So Starving

According to *BusinessWeek* magazine, the second-best place for artists is Santa Fe, New Mexico. Several factors were used to find the best places: population diversity, percentage of people between twenty-five and thirty-four, and the number of museums, orchestras, theater troupes, library resources, and college arts programs. Those factors combined made Los Angeles number one for artists.

Santa Fe has a blending of new and the traditional Native American and Hispanic heritages. The community has a large number of creative individuals, artistic businesses, and over 12,500 jobs in the creative industry. In turn, Santa Fe's creative industry represents 17.5 percent of their total employment. Santa Fe has the largest per capita concentration of writers, performers, and artists of any city in the entire United States. In terms of total dollar sales, Santa Fe is the second-largest art market in America and the highest per capita of art-related businesses in the country. Santa Fe is also the first city in the United States to be named to the UNESCO Creative Cities list.

O'Keeffe Country

The famous American artist Georgia O'Keeffe adopted New Mexico as her permanent home in 1929. And the city permanently adopted her with the opening of the Georgia O'Keeffe Museum in Santa Fe in 1997. Of the nearly 3,000 pieces in its collection, 1,154 are O'Keeffe's. The museum's permanent collection of her work is the largest in the world.

45 The Second-Most-Visited Website in the United States:

Oh, My Yahoo!

The giant Internet search engine Google is probably pretty annoyed that the second-most-visited website is Yahoo!, with 470 million unique visitors.

Yahoo! had its beginning as a student hobby for two PhD candidates in electrical engineering at Stanford University, David Filo and Jerry Yang. It was February 1994 when they developed a guide to help them track their personal interests on the Internet. Soon, the duo was devoting more and more time and energy to their guide to their favorite sites than on their doctoral dissertations—imagine that! Then, the lists became monstrously long and confusing, so the men decided to break them into categories. When those became too large, they developed specific subcategories, which became the main concept of Yahoo!. Their original name, like many firsts, was not quite as cool. It was, "Jerry and David's Guide to the World Wide Web." Fortunately, with the help of a dictionary, they found the name *Yahoo!*, an acronym for "Yet Another Hierarchical Officious Oracle." However, they much preferred the general definition of a "yahoo" as being "rude, unsophisticated, and uncouth."

Google recently announced that Facebook, with more than 540 million unique visitors and grabbing 35 percent of all Internet users, is the most visited site on the web.

> **Ya-whew!**
> After they shared their guide format with others in the Stanford community, the word spread so fast that Yahoo! reached its first million-hit day in the fall of the same year it launched.

The Second-Longest Word in English:

Sad Word, Happy Word

The second-longest word in the English language is a happy word that kids love the challenge of saying: *supercalifragilisticexpialidocious*. This fun word is thirty-four letters long, and if Mary Poppins is to be believed, it can make you feel happy just saying the word. Up until 1964, when the word was introduced to the American public, the longest and hardest word for children to say was "antidisestablishmentarianism." We can all thank the Disney musical movie *Mary Poppins* for the song "Supercalifragilisticexpialidocious," as well as the ensuing headaches whenever stuck watching the movie with youngsters.

The longest word in English is *pneumonoultramicscopicsilicovolcanoconiosis*, which is forty-three letters long. It is a lung disease that is caused by inhaling microscopic volcanic dust particles deep inside a person's lungs and, by the time it takes you to spell (or even pronounce) what you've got, you're already dead.

More Long Words

- The longest word with all the vowels in order: *pancreaticoduodenostomy*
- The longest word where all the letters appear twice: *esophagographers*
- The word with the longest run of vowels: *queuing*
- The word with the longest run of consonants: *latchstring*
- The longest word with just one vowel: *strengths*
- The longest word to alternate consonants and vowels: *honorificabilitudinitatibus*
- The longest word in alphabetical order: *aegilops*
- The longest words without repeating letter: *uncopyrightable* and *dermatoglyphics*

The Second Top Single Record:

The Crosby Show

The second-bestselling single record in the world is, with more than 30,000,000 singles sold, Bing Crosby's "White Christmas," released in 1942. "White Christmas" was written by Irving Berlin for the 1942 musical motion picture *Holiday Inn*. The song was awarded an Academy Award for the Song of the Year in 1942.

We all know that Hollywood loves to repeat itself, but things got a little out of control with Bing and his song. First, in the 1946 movie *Blue Skies*, Bing Crosby sang "White Christmas" for a second time. Then, in 1954, it was the theme of the movie *White Christmas*. What made the seasonal song such a huge hit? Perhaps it was because the song was originally released during the height of World War II, and it reminded Americans of simpler times—when nothing could top a snowfall at Christmas to share with family and friends inside a warm house with a log on the fire and conversations about mystical elves.

The bestselling single record in the world is Sir Elton John's "Candle in the Wind" (1997), with sales in excess of 37,000,000. It is also a second in that it is actually an updated version of the 1973 song that Elton John recorded in memory of Marilyn Monroe. The second, more popular version was recorded in memory of the late Diana, Princess of Wales.

I'm Dreaming of a New Beginning

Born Israel Beilin, Irving Berlin was born in nineteenth-century Russia in a Jewish shtetl. His family later immigrated to the United States. His father died when he was thirteen, and Berlin had to sing for pennies in the streets of New York to help support his family. But all that practice would pay off as he went on to write more than 1,200 songs and live to be 100 years old.

48

The Artist with the Second Most Grammy Awards:

"Fly Me to the Moon"

He may not take the gold medal, but he has a lot of gold records. Quincy Jones comes in second with twenty-seven Grammy awards to his name. Jones collected his first Grammy for his Count Basie arrangement of "I Can't Stop Loving You" in 1963. One of his arrangements was out of this world, literally: "Fly Me to the Moon" was played on the moon's surface by astronaut Buzz Aldrin in 1969. While he might be number two on the number of awards won, Quincy is the tops when it comes to the most Grammy nominations with a total of seventy-nine nominations.

In addition to all of his Grammy awards, Quincy has received the French Ministry of Culture's Distinguished Arts and Letters Award, the coveted Polar Music Prize from Sweden, and the Rudolph Valentino Award for the Republic of Italy. Jones has also received honorary doctorates from fourteen different universities and institutions. He was named the 2001 Kennedy Center Honoree for his contribution to the culture of America. The diversity of music he has influenced—from hip-hop to classic—is as impressive as the number of awards he's received.

The artist with the most Grammy awards with thirty-one is the British conductor Sir Georg Solti.

We Are the Eagles

Quincy was the driving force as the producer and conductor behind the historic song "We Are the World." He also frequently worked with Michael Jackson, including on his bestselling album of all-time, *Thriller*. *Thriller* may lead the world, but it places second in the United States to the Eagles' album *Their Greatest Hits, 1971–1975*. Considering how many people actually buy albums today, these records might be set in stone.

Underground Sugar Supplier

If you're like most Americans, you probably spend more time thinking about when you're going to get your next hit of sugar than where it actually comes from. Lurking underground is a hidden, second sugar source: the sugar beet, supplying the world with 30 percent of its sugar. Cane sugar supplies the other 70 percent.

But aren't beets purple and pickled? The beets preferred at Schrute Farms are. But the sugar beet is a biennial plant that spends its entire first year storing food (sugar) in its roots to fuel its production of flowers and seeds in its second year. However, beet farmers harvest most of their beets during their first year while they're packed full of sugar. The sugar beet actually has a higher sugar content (17 percent) than cane sugar (10 percent).

Today's sugar beets have their roots in the sea beet that grew around the Black and Mediterranean Seas. It was domesticated and spread throughout Europe. During the Napoleonic Wars, after Britain blockaded sugar from getting to continental Europe, Napoleon increased the planting of the sugar beet. Turnabout is fair play: during the World War I, Britain's sugar import supply was threatened, so the Brits started growing sugar beets of their own.

Just Beet It

- Sugar was once presented in jewel-studded boxes to European royalty.
- The American consumer eats an average of 45 pounds of sugar annually.
- In the early 1980s *Sesame Street* introduced the sugar beet song, which only had two words, "sugar beet," and was sung weekly.
- There are 10,000 beet farmers in the United States and Canada, including the fictional and aforementioned Schrute Farms, popularized on the American version of NBC's *The Office*.

Trying to Catch Up

Times are changing; and so are the condiments. After a thirteen-year reign as the bestselling condiment, ketchup now comes in second. The number one selling condiment today? Salsa. However, since ketchup is found in more than 97 percent of the U.S. kitchens, it's considered the most widely used condiment. The first ketchup was not your mother's ketchup, it didn't even contain tomatoes; it began as a sauce of anchovies, walnuts, mushrooms, and kidney beans.

The word ketchup is thought to have derived from *koechiap* or *ke-tsiap*, which means brine of picked fish or shellfish in the Amoy dialect of China. Present-day Worcestershire sauce would be a closer match to ancient ketchup. From China, the "ketchup" migrated to Malaysia and Indonesia and then to England by sailors. In the early 1700s, Spaniards living in Mexico mixed the tomato into their ketchup and the idea spread to Europe. In 1876, the Heinz Company started the production of tomato ketchup and just called it "ketchup." Today, there are more than sixty kinds of ketchup, and it's one of the few processed foods containing no preservatives.

Ketchup Is a Tasty Treat

Ketchup's popularity might be because of its ability to stimulate all five known palatable senses—sweet, salty, sour, bitter, and umami—of the tongue. Umami is the newly discovered taste found in cured meat, chicken soup, mother's milk, seaweed, and cooked tomatoes. Ketchup is 25 percent sugar, so maybe that's why it has been so popular.

The Second-Oldest Toy:

I've Got the World on a String

The second-oldest toy has seen a lot of ups and downs and has been around for more than 2,500 years: the Yo-Yo. But it wasn't always called a Yo-Yo. Early Greek children played with wooden ones and some believe that the Chinese might have been yo-yoing even earlier. The Yo-Yo came to England in the 1800s where it adopted many names, bandalore, quiz, whirl-a-gig, and a Prince of Wales toy, to name a few. In the 1860s, the Yo-Yo came to America, but the word *Yo-Yo* wasn't heard until 1920, when Pedro Flores, a Philippine immigrant, started mass-producing them in a factory in California with the Yo-Yo name. Later, Donald Duncan came along to see the toy. He ended up buying the rights from Flores and trademarked the name Yo-Yo. Duncan improved the Yo-Yo's design with a slip string, allowing for tricks like the "sleep." In 1962, Yo-Yo sales peaked with more than 45 million sold. The Yo-Yo can claim to be a toy that is out of this world because it has the distinction of being the first toy in space. When it comes to number one, girls rule here. The oldest toy by most accounts is the doll.

Yo! A $500 Yo-Yo
This is a far stretch from the first wooden Yo-Yo. The Freehand Mg is a $500, 99 percent pure magnesium, 1 percent magnesium chemical stabilizer Yo-Yo. The Yo-Yo body is forged individually and smoothed by a computer-controlled lathe to 1/100,000-of-an-inch tolerance. It has ceramic bearings that are five to ten times smoother than steel.

Dream On

No one remembers the winner of the third season of *Britain's Got Talent*. But everyone remembers the second-place winner: Susan Boyle.

Susan, a singer, came on the show as a forty-eight-year-old church volunteer from a small, Scottish village outside of Edinburgh. She was not the usual contestant for the show because of her age, frumpy appearance, and frizzy hair; however, her incredible voice visibly shocked the three judges, Simon Cowell, Piers Morgan, and Amanda Holden—not to mention the entire studio and viewing audiences. In the finals, Susan spruced up her appearance with a glamorous, floor-length dress and a soft coloring of her hair. Boyle sang the song that made her famous and an instant, viral YouTube star, "I Dreamed the Dream" from the musical *Les Miserables*. Millions of Brits watched the final show and voted by telephone afterward; most thought Susan would win easily. However, the show is as much a popularity contest as it is a talent show, and Diversity, a dance act, bested Boyle. But the true reason she came in second probably lies in the fact that, because so many people figured Susan was a shoo-in to win, they didn't bother to vote.

Britain's Got Talent Facts

- Susan Boyle's debut album set a record as the world's bestselling album in 2009.
- In the first week of sales, season one winner, Paul Potts, had his debut album sell more copies than all the top ten combined.

Gone to the Dogs

The Dickin Medal is named after Maria Dickin, founder of a British veterinary charity. The award is given to animals that display bravery and devotion while serving in the British armed forces or civil emergency services. The second-most-decorated species, with 19 Dickin Medals, is the dog. A white mongrel dog named Bob was the first dog to get the medal. Bob was on a night patrol with a British infantry unit when he froze and refused to move, indicating a nearby enemy ambush. Most of the dogs received their medals during World War II, but after September 11, 2001, three dogs were given the award for their role in the response to the terrorist attacks that day. Salty and Roselle were guide dogs who directed their blind owners (along with several others) down more than seventy flights of stairs to safety; a New York Police Department dog, Apollo, was given the award for his tireless rescue efforts to find victims of the attack.

The animal receiving the most Dickin Awards is the pigeon, with thirty-two medals for carrying messages during World War II.

The Famous Feline

Able Seacat Simon is the only cat to receive the Dickin Medal. Simon was wounded in an attack on the HMS *Amethyst* that killed seventeen men. Simon continued bravely to kill off an infestation of rats that were eating the sailors' meager rations while the ship was held captive during the notorious Yangtze Incident of World War II.

The Second Toy Erector Set:

Young Engineers

The second toy erector set was the creation of Dr. A. C. Gilbert, one of the most multi-talented inventors in the world. One day, Dr. Gilbert decided to make a construction kit for kids with evenly spaced holes for bolts, screws, pulleys, gears, and even engines. Gilbert knew about the erector set invented by Frank Hornby in 1901 called "Mechanics Made Easy," but Gilbert's erector set was much more realistic, with 90-degree angles so that four of them could be joined together to form a stable, square, and hollow base.

In 1913, Gilbert marketed his "Mysto Erector Structural Steel Builder." With a name like that, combined with the first major American ad campaign for a toy, the good doctor's erector set became the most desired toy on the market. Soon, living rooms were changed into miniature cities. In 1962, Gilbert's rival in the erector toy business, British firm Meccano, purchased the rights to his erector set and sell them today.

The Amazing Alfred Carlton Gilbert

In addition to being a toy inventor, Carlton Gilbert won a gold medal in pole-vaulting in the Olympiad in London. He made some of the finest model trains ever made, a glass blowing kit, a chemical set (in 1958, one that was especially made for girls), and even an "Atomic Energy Lab" with real radioactive materials and a working Geiger counter.

Top Tongue Tormentors

Finally, in our world of rating things, there is a rating scale for the spiciest peppers called the Scoville Scale, which rates peppers by Scoville Heat Units (SHU). The second hottest is the Red Savina Pepper (SHU:350,000–580,000). The Red Savina is in the habanero family and is nicknamed the "Dominican Devil's Tongue Pepper" and the "Ball of Fire Pepper." The Red Savina is twice as hot as the regular habanero pepper and sixty-five times the strength of the jalapeño pepper. Adding 1 gram of the Red Savina can produce noticeable heat in 1,272 pounds of sauce. The full strength, 100 percent Red Savina isn't even sold to minors because of its strength. The Red Savina was developed by Frank Garica when he noticed a red fruited habanero plant in the midst of a field of orange fruited habaneros. Garcia harvested the seeds from the newly found red one and the Red Savina was born. Garcia received a Plant Variety Protection (good for 18 years) for his Red Savinas in 1993 from the U.S. Department of Agriculture. The hottest pepper on the scale, with a rating of 1,041,427 Scoville Heat Units (SHU) is the Naja Jolokia pepper—aka, the Ghost Pepper—from Bangladash.

Is There Pepper in Pepper Spray?
Most police forces have pepper spray in their arsenal of non-lethal weapons. Pepper spray does contain capsaicin, which is the active ingredient in hot peppers. Pure capsaicin has a SHU rating of 15,000,000 to 16,000,000, while police pepper spray holds a 5,000,000 to 5,300,000 SHU rating.

Tipsy Italians

It's no wonder that Italians are the second-greatest consumers of wine, with the average Italian putting away 80.4 pints annually. Italians live in the greatest wine-producing country in the world, where they have been making wine for more than 2,800 years! Italy produces more than 7 billion bottles of wine annually, and Italy's wine output is among the most diverse in the world.

Some of the wines take the names of the towns of where they were produced, such as Barolo, Amarone, Soave, Fiano di Avellino, and Mad Dog 20/20. Italy's landmass is 80 percent hills or mountains, which makes for ideal conditions for growing vineyards. Most of the wine is produced along the Chianti River, which runs along more than a hundred towns in six provinces. Italians have a strong tradition of craftsmanship in the areas of cars, shoes, food, art, architecture, and opera, and they apply that same craftsmanship to their wine.

Luxembourg is the country with the greatest consumers of wine per capita. Luxembourgians put away 110.2 pints of wine per year.

What's in a Name?
Not all Italian wines are named after their towns. Many are named after the variety of grapes used to make them instead. So a particular variety of wine might be excellent in one place, yet inferior in another, depending on the grapes used rather than the location in which they were grown.

Chocoholics

One of the smallest countries in Europe has the biggest hunger for chocolate. The Principality of Liechtenstein, sandwiched between Switzerland and Austria, has the second-highest per capita consumption at twenty-four pounds. The greatest chocolate consumers are the Brits, with an annual per capita fix of 25.4 pounds—an average of a little more than an ounce a day. Liechtenstein does have the highest gross national product per capita in the world; maybe it's all of that extra disposable income that allows them to indulge in their constant chocolate cravings.

The Mayans of Mexico and Central America were the first to consume chocolate in the form of an invigorating drink made with cacao beans ground up into a powder and mixed with water. The Mayans made the drink for their privileged classes more than 2,000 years ago. Chocolate later came to be consumed in the solid form of a chocolate bar. Joseph Fry, an Englishman, gets credit for making the first chocolate bar in 1847, while Daniel Peter, of Switzerland, developed milk chocolate in 1876 using condensed milk created by Henri Nestle.

Food of the Gods Facts

- The famous "Father of Taxonomy," Carl Linnaeus, named the cacao tree *Theobroma cacao*, which means "cacao, food of the gods."
- A tiny, gnat-like midge pollinates the flowers of the cacao tree, and only about 10 percent of pollinated flowers grow into the cacao fruit (cacao bean).

Please Squeeze Me

The good ol' U.S.A is the second-greatest orange producer, with more than 8,109,704 tons of oranges grown a year. Within the United States, Florida produces more oranges than any other state. Brazil is the greatest orange-producing country, with an annual yield of about 20,149,489 tons.

Have you ever eaten a mutant? You do every time you eat a navel orange. This fortunate "mutant" was discovered in 1820 in an orange plantation in Brazil. The navel orange has a feature on one side that looks like a human bellybutton, or navel. However, within the "navel" of the navel orange is a underdeveloped conjoined twin orange surrounded by the rind of its seedless twin. In 1870, the USDA approved the introduction of the navel orange into the United States. The first place where the Brazilian navel orange trees were planted in the United States was in Riverside, California, in 1873. Three trees were planted, and one is still alive today, producing fruit. Since the navel oranges are seedless, they can only propagate by grafting the branch of a navel orange tree to another orange tree. Amazingly, all navel oranges originate from a single Brazilian navel orange tree.

Facts You Orange to Know

- A very rare variety of the navel orange is the Cara Cara orange. It has a reddish, pink flesh and a faint taste of strawberries.
- Columbus brought orange seeds to America to grow orange trees.
- Oranges will not overripen if left on the tree.

PART 2

Historical Number Twos

If history is a race, then what's the prize?

Perhaps because there is so damned much history, in our attempts to grasp it all, we rarely grab onto much beyond the surface—the first to discover, the first to invent, the first to conquer. But what about those silver medal inventors and conquerors? Are those who are first the only ones who accomplish? Why not take a second look at the things from our past that have propelled us to today?

The fact that some event happens second in history does not diminish its worth or importance. It's like historical procrastination: the times, the people, and the circumstances did not allow it to happen sooner. The second time an event occurs can change the direction of a nation's history and its citizens' way of thinking and dealing with their problems. Just think: what will be the next part of our history to be written with seconds?

Sometimes, the Second Time Is the Charm

For better or worse, Americans have long been using their Constitution and what they believe to have been the true intentions of their founding fathers to shape their thoughts and choices. This seems like a pretty radical approach to reading, considering the founding fathers couldn't even get the words right the first time. The U.S. Constitution as it is known and commented on today is not even the United States' original constitution. The first Constitution (The Articles of Confederation and Perpetual Union) was drafted in 1777 at the Second Continental Congress and completely ratified by 1781. But in 1787, in response to a growing call for a stronger, central government, the United States adopted its second (and, so far, last) Constitution.

All debate aside, this second Constitution has served the United States remarkably well for the past 223 years. This is especially true if you consider just how many constitutions other countries have gone through. In particular, consider the year when each of these countries' current constitution was ratified: Italy (1947), France (1958), Serbia (2006), North Korea (2009), South Korea (1948), Japan (1947), Egypt (1971), Greece (1975), and Brazil (1988).

If Brevity Is the Art of Wit, Alabama Is Coloring Way Outside of the Lines
The U.S. Constitution is the world's oldest and shortest functioning Constitution. The same cannot be said about Alabama's state constitution. Unlike the succinctness of the U.S. Constitution, this state's constitution is about twelve times longer than most state constitutions. How were they able to pull this feat off? By amending it over 800 times (and counting).

The United States' Second Declared War:

Mexicans of Mass Destruction

In his plea to congress for a declaration of war on Mexico, President James K. Polk asserted, "... after reiterated menaces, Mexico has passed the boundary of the United States, has invaded our territory and shed American blood upon the American soil. She has proclaimed that hostilities have commenced, and that the two nations are now at war."

As far as Mexicans "invading" the United States, Mexico claimed it was reacting to invading Americans. The problem was that Americans claimed that the Rio Grande River served as their border with Mexico, while the Mexicans held that the border was 150 miles farther north at the Nueces River. The ensuing confusion was what Polk had wanted. Committed to the idea of the United States' Manifest Destiny, Polk's reasons for going to war had less to do with protecting America's borders than it did with expanding them. Thus, the reasons behind going to war were not nearly as important as securing legitimacy for it. Once Mexico "invaded" Texas, the United States had its excuse to expand. In the end, the United States gained land that would become the states of California, Arizona, and New Mexico. Mexico, conversely, was reduced to nearly half its size.

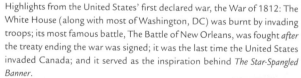

War! What Is It Good For?

Highlights from the United States' first declared war, the War of 1812: The White House (along with most of Washington, DC) was burnt by invading troops; its most famous battle, The Battle of New Orleans, was fought *after* the treaty ending the war was signed; it was the last time the United States invaded Canada; and it served as the inspiration behind *The Star-Spangled Banner*.

Depends on What the Meaning of "Seconds" Is

When the William J. Clinton Presidential Library opened in November 18, 2004, it was the largest Presidential Library, with 68,698 square feet of floor space. The second largest was the Ronald Reagan Presidential Library. But in October 2005, the Air Force One Pavilion was completed to house Reagan's 707 Air Force One plane, flying this second into first. The pavilion added an extra 90,000 square feet, giving the library a total area of about 153,000 square feet.

Bumped to second by an airplane, the Clinton Library still soars above all Presidential Libraries when it comes to what's on the inside: 2 million photographs, 80 million pages of documents, and 79,000 artifacts. The Clinton Library is the first to house electronic information, including 21 million e-mails. It has an exact replica of the Oval Office, right down to the last cigar. Located in Little Rock, Arkansas, overlooking the Arkansas River, it is the most expensive Presidential Library. Amazingly, though, it was built completely on private donations rather than using public funds. And charging stations in the parking lot for electric vehicles, flooring made of recycled tires, and solar panels on the roof are just a few features that make it the greenest Presidential Library.

Presidential Library Facts

- The smallest Presidential Library is Herbert Hoover's in West Branch, Iowa.
- Formal Presidential Libraries began with Franklin D. Roosevelt in 1939, when he donated his presidential papers to the federal government along with some property at his Hyde Park place to build a library and museum.
- Most presidents are buried on the grounds of their Presidential Libraries.

The Size of Central Park

The second-smallest country, Monaco, could fit inside New York City's Central Park. But its seconds don't end there; with a density of 43,000 people per square mile, Monaco rolls in behind fellow gambling hotspot, Macau, as the second-most-densely populated country in the world.

Before close to 100 acres of the sea were reclaimed, Monaco was even smaller. Still, it's only a little less than four football fields wide at its narrowest point. Monaco had its beginning one night in 1297, when François Grimaldi pretended to be a monk and led a few soldiers to overcome the fortress guarding the Rock of Monaco. The principality has been ruled by the princes of the Grimaldi family for the last 700 years. In more recent history, Monaco gained independence from France in 1861 when it gave France half of its land. However, the ruling prince did not realize that he gave his best land away. In order to make up for his blunder, the prince decided to use gambling as a means to support the economy of the country. Monaco remains a highly desired gambling destination to this day.

Deus Ex Machina

The world's smallest country, Vatican City, is a walled country inside Rome. It is home to the Catholic Church and ruled by the Pope. Vatican City was created in 1927 in a treaty between the dictator, Benito Mussolini, and the Pope. The country does not have any street addresses or permanent citizens, but it does have ATM machines that are in Italian and Latin.

Oh, Secanada!

S kating into the number two spot with 3.9 million square miles is Canada, little more than half the size of landmass leader, Russia, which boasts 6.6 million square miles. But, as we've all been told, it's not size that matters—it's what you do with your landmass that counts. While much of Russia consists of poor soil and even poorer weather conditions (either too hot or too cold) for agriculture, Canada makes the most of its immensity: with hundreds of thousands of square miles of surface water within its border, Canada owns the podium when it comes to getting wet. In fact, a full quarter of the world's freshwater is found in Canada. Canada is also home to one-quarter of the wetlands on the planet and ranks third in the amount of glaciers behind Antarctica and Greenland. There are 3 million lakes and 30 million people in Canada; that means there is one lake for every ten Canadians (roughly one per hockey team). Permafrost covers about 55 percent of Canada, most of it in the northern regions of Canada.

Cool Canadian Facts

- Canada has the world's largest freshwater island, Manitoulin Island, in Lake Huron.
- Mt. Everest may be the tallest mountain, but Canada's Mount Logan is believed to have the largest footprint of any known mountain massif.
- Canada ranks fourth in lowest population density with three people for every square kilometer.
- Canada has the longest national highway in the world, the Trans-Canada Highway, with a distance of 4,725 miles.
- Canada holds the world record for the longest coastline, with 125,570 miles of coast.
- The United States buys more oil from Canada than from Saudi Arabia.

The Tallest Second

L ocated in California and established in 1890, Sequoia National Park is the second-oldest national park in America. It's better known for enormous sequoias than for gushing geysers. In fact, five of the tallest trees in the world are found growing in Sequoia National Park. The General Sherman Tree holds the record for the largest tree in the world based on sheer volume. By the best estimates, The Sherman Tree has a total volume of 52,500 cubic feet. The Sherman Tree has a maximum diameter of 36.5 feet and rises 275 feet above the ground. There is enough room around the tree for about fifty people to stand side by side. The park is also home to the highest point in the continental United States, Mt. Whitney (elevation: 14,491 feet above sea level). About 84 percent of the park is classified as a wilderness area and can only be reached by foot, horseback, or tree swing.

The very first national park in the world was Yellowstone, established in 1872. Situated mainly in Wyoming, it spills over to areas of Idaho and Montana. It's home to many extraordinary hot spring geysers, the most famous being Old Faithful.

Sequoia Stuff

- Sequoia wood is so brittle that some trees shatter when they hit the ground.
- Sequoia National Park and its sister park, Kings Canyon, contain more than 200 caves, including the longest cave in California, Lilburn Cave.
- Sometimes, one may see a near perfect line of four or five sequoias. Scientists believe that as a fallen sequoia decays, seedlings find success, sprouting along the rich organic material it leaves behind.

The Right to Bear Others' Opinions

F ew amendments to the U.S. Constitution have been under as much scrutiny as its second. In search of supportive evidence, advocates often aim abroad to gather ammo for their arguments.

Switzerland is often bandied about as the paragon for a packing public. Not only is it legal for Swiss citizens to possess firearms, but they are obligated to do so. Rather than paying for a full army to sit around, the Swiss have decided to take a "we'll call you when we need you" approach to military readiness. Whether it's the cause for or result of this policy, Switzerland has become as synonymous with neutrality as it is with yodeling. Who would vote for war if it meant *everyone* had to fight? Who would invade if they knew *everyone* was strapped? The Swiss refer to this last question as the "porcupine" approach: a society of armed citizens would be like a collection of quills to any potential invaders. But if the government is giving its citizens guns (in addition to regulating and training citizens how to use them) in the name of military readiness, is that an example of decreased or increased governmental gun control?

A Second Shot

The Second Amendment wasn't really second. Actually, it's part of the Bill of Rights. The Bill of Rights is a collection of the original ten amendments. They were passed as a single bill rather than ten separate amendments. Thus, the right to bear arms wasn't the second alteration to the U.S. Constitution. That honor goes to the 11th Amendment, ratified four years after the Bill of Rights.

America's True Ironman

The statue of Vulcan, the Roman god of fire, is a true "Ironman" because it is made of cast iron. The statue is of Vulcan with a spear in his left hand and a hammer resting on an anvil in his right. It stands 56 feet tall (the height of a five-story building), holds the record for the largest cast iron statue in the world, and now makes its home in Birmingham, Alabama. The Vulcan had its beginning as an exhibit in the 1904 St. Louis World's Fair. To symbolize Birmingham's leadership in the production of iron, the Commercial Club of Birmingham commissioned the construction of Vulcan. After the fair closed, Vulcan was shipped back to Birmingham, where it lay in pieces for many years. In 1936, Vulcan was put back together and placed in Vulcan Park where it can still be seen there today.

As for number one? Well apparently, "Lady Liberty" is just her stage name. Her given name? The Statue of Liberty Enlightening the World. Regardless what name she goes by, this French gift is the largest statue in America. From the ground to the tip of her flame, the Statue of Liberty is 305 feet and 1 inch tall—about the size of a twenty-two-story building.

Statue Secret
The Statue of Liberty has at least one secret that only a few people know. The statue's feet have a broken chain wrapped around them that visitors cannot see from the ground. The broken chain juts out from under her robe and symbolizes her freedom to move forward.

No Objections, Your Honor

For most of its existence, the U.S. Supreme Court truly has been the "court of the last resort" when it came to minority justices. Today, we live in unique times: currently, the second-ever woman *and* second-ever African American are serving on the bench along with the first-ever Hispanic, Sonia Sotomayor.

As remarkable as being the second woman appointed to the court is, it may not even be Ruth Bader Ginsburg's most amazing achievement. She's the only person to have made law review at both Harvard and Columbia law schools. But school was always secondary. Just fourteen months before she started law school at Harvard, Bader Ginsburg gave birth to her first child. The ever-devoted mother and wife, Bader Ginsburg left Harvard Law School after two years of study when her husband got a job in New York City. While she was determined to get her law degree, keeping her family together proved to be an even higher priority.

Justice Clarence Thomas is only the second African American to serve on the Supreme Court. But he almost went on to serve an even higher power. Thomas initially studied to become a priest before dropping out to study English at Holy Cross and later attend Yale Law School.

Where's the Respect?

Although Bader Ginsburg is a long-time champion of women's rights, it might be her dissenting opinion in the case, *Bush v. Gore*, for which she will be remembered most. When it was her turn to deliver her decision during the Court's majority ruling in favor of George W. Bush, Bader Ginsburg simply stated: "I dissent." What stood out wasn't her position as much as her omission of the word "respectfully" in it.

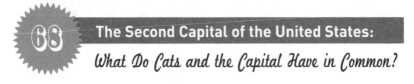
Apparently, they have the same number of lives. Starting with Philadelphia in 1776, the seat of America's government switched cities nine times before settling on Washington, DC. Philadelphia was the original site of the capital, but Baltimore was the first stop on its one-time U.S. tour.

The delegates of the Continental Congress didn't make the move for the crabcakes. The move was more of a retreat from the British troops advancing on Philadelphia. In fact, as soon as the coast was clear, just four months later, the delegates moved the capital right back to Philly—that is, before they hit the road again, making stops in Lancaster, Pennsylvania; York, Pennsylvania; Princeton, New Jersey; Annapolis, Maryland; Trenton, New Jersey; New York, New York; and, finally, Washington, DC. Since the country didn't really become the United States until its second constitution was ratified in 1787, New York City (the location of the capital at the time) could be considered *this* nation's first capital, with Washington, DC, as its second.

Compromising Locations

If the capital was constantly on the move, what got it to stop? Compromise. Even though it would be more than seventy years before the country would fall into civil war, social and economic divisions had been there from the start. Thus, the founding fathers found a compromise. The capital would go between two Southern slave states (Maryland and Virginia). In return, the North got the Southern votes necessary to pass a bill establishing the federal assumption of state debts.

The Second-Least Populous Country:

Here Today, Gone Tomorrow

The second-least populous country, Tuvalu, is surrounded by water. Situated in the South Pacific, about 600 miles north of Fiji and east of Australia, Tuvalu is made of six true atolls and three reef islands. With a total land area of ten square miles, this island nation is number four on the list of smallest (by landmass) countries in the world.

If global warming and rising sea levels persist, low-lying Tuvalu could be the first sovereign nation to become uninhabitable within the next fifty years, making its 12,576 citizens the first environmental refugees on the planet. But Tuvalu isn't sitting back as it sinks. It's taking steps in establishing renewable sources of energy. It has a bio-gas digester that produces cooking gas from the manure of pigs with plans to make a second bio-gas generator to handle human waste and other trash.

With a current population of 826 people, Vatican City leads the world as the least populated country in the world.

The World's First $50 Million TV

Not long after Tuvalu was assigned its Internet country code, TV entrepreneur Jason Chapnik thought it would be an excellent code for registering names. But unlike the others who contacted the Tuvalu government, Jason chose to visit Tuvalu with his wife instead of his business partners to make his pitch. Seeing that Jason was a family man impressed the government enough to sway them to award him the control of the domain name. His $50 million offer didn't hurt his case either.

The Largest Isn't a No-Brainer

With a total of 145 million items (over 33 million books, 3 million recordings, more than 12.5 million photographs, 6 million pieces of sheet music, and 63 million manuscripts) the shelves at the U.S. Library of Congress are certainly stacked, but is it the biggest library on the planet?

The leading contender for number two is the British Library in London. With over 150 million items, the British Library holds about 14 million books, some dating back as far as 300 B.C. So, why the confusion as to who's bigger? If the British Library has 5 million more items, it's the largest, right? It depends on what you measure. While the British Library might have more stuff, it has less space. When it comes to shelf mileage, the U.S. Library of Congress has the advantage at 540 miles to 388. So, which is first and which is second? It depends on if you're into depth or distance.

Not-So-Mobile Maps

Some of the British Library's most treasured items are the Magna Carta and Leonardo da Vinci's notebook. The library also has a copy of the largest atlas ever made: the 350-year-old Klencke Atlas. It's 5 feet 9 inches high and 6 feet 3 inches wide and has just recently been open for public viewing. There isn't a whole lot of concern about someone trying to "borrow" the big book for their next road trip; it weighs so much that six people are needed to carry it. The British Library, a combination of several institutions into one library, is relatively new, with the Queen formally opening it in 1998.

A Second Chance for Sumatran Rhinos

In 1875, the Cincinnati Zoo and Botanical Garden became the country's second zoo. When it first opened, the zoo exhibited just eight monkeys, six raccoons, three deer, two grizzly bears, two elk, a buffalo, a tiger, a hyena, an alligator, a circus elephant, and several hundred birds. Currently, the Cincinnati Zoo has 500 animals and 3,000 plant species in its collections. It also just pulls ahead of the Philadelphia Zoo with 1.2 million visitors a year. What animal lovers like most about the zoo is the second chance for existence it's given some species. Its captive breeding program for the critically endangered Sumatran rhinos is the only successful one in the world.

Philadelphia is responsible for many firsts in the history of the United States, including its first zoo. The Philadelphia Zoo hosted 813 animals and 228,000 visitors during its first year. Today, the zoo has about 1,300 animals and 1.1 million annual visitors. The charter to establish the zoo was signed in 1859, but the commencement of the Civil War caused the realization of the zoo to be delayed until 1874. Yet it still took first by a year.

Are You Dung with That Paper?
An elephant eats around 500 pounds of food a day and dooks out about 100 pounds. Some even make paper from its poop because it is so fiber-rich. The dung is first washed and boiled, then laid out to dry. It's estimated that one elephant can pinch out 115 sheets of paper. What's amazing is that dung from a healthy elephant doesn't smell bad...or so we're told.

The First Crack in the Union

Ratifying the U.S. Constitution in 1787, Pennsylvania became the second colony after Delaware to become a state in the United States of America. But Pennsylvania should be just as well known for what it denied as for what it helped establish. Its southern border, shared with Maryland, was first drawn to settle a dispute between two feuding families: the Calverts of Maryland and the Penns of . . . duh. This feud got so heated that, in the 1730s, it spawned Cresap's War. It wasn't until Charles Mason and Jeremiah Dixon surveyed the disputed territories between 1763 and 1767 that both sides had a boundary they could live with.

Little did the Calverts or Penns know this line would go on to become as much or more of a symbol for the country than for their families. The Mason-Dixon Line, as it went on to be known, wound up serving as a line demarcating a legal and cultural split in the United States. With the Missouri Compromise of 1820, slavery was abolished for states above it and retained for those below it.

English as a Second Language

To many of Pennsylvania's most popular residents—the Amish and the Mennonites—English is their second language. Their first language is a variation of German called Pennsylvanian Dutch. Yep, the "Dutch" they speak is actually German. Why? Because the German word for German is *Deutsch*, which for many English speakers comes out as "Dutch." And, that's how you get Dutch Germans and Pennsylvanian Dutch.

We'll Always Have Swinoujscie

If it hadn't been for one man's unconquerable lighthouse love, the Cape Hatteras Lighthouse in the United States would now be the tallest brick lighthouse in the world. Instead, it remains the second-tallest brick lighthouse by only 13 feet. The Cape Hatteras Lighthouse is located on North Carolina's Outer Banks and is affectionately called "The Grand Lady of Lighthouses." The lighthouse is made of over one million bricks, and it took two years to build. It was completed in 1870 and is the tallest lighthouse in the United States, at 200 feet. Even with the lighthouse, more than 1,000 ships have been lost off Cape Hatteras, causing it to be known as "The Graveyard of the Atlantic."

At 213 feet high, Poland's Swinoujscie Lighthouse along the Baltic Sea is the world's tallest brick lighthouse. It was almost destroyed during the World War II by retreating Germans. But like the plot of some absurdist, war movie romance, the German soldier stationed in the lighthouse to work as its keeper had grown too attached to it. In the end, he couldn't bring himself to ignite the fuses rigged to destroy his object of affection.

How Do You Move a 200-Foot-High Lighthouse?
Very carefully. The Cape Hatteras Lighthouse was actually moved 2,870 feet inland to safer ground because of beach erosion around the original site. Many were concerned that the move would cause the 130-year-old lighthouse to break apart, but it was successfully moved in twenty-three days by the International Chimney Corporation of Buffalo and Expert House Movers of Maryland.

The Second-Tallest Brick Building in the World:

Now with 22-Foot-Thick Walls!

The second-tallest brick building is the Philadelphia City Hall. It's so tall that it has 22-foot-thick base walls in order to hold up the massive weight of its 548-foot-tall structure. Most masonry buildings have a steel framework with bricks or stone cladding on the outside. Not so with the Philadelphia City Hall; the 88 million handmade bricks in the building are joined directly to each other as opposed to being held in place by an overall structure. The City Hall is the first at a couple of things: it's the tallest load-bearing building in the world and it's the largest municipal building in America with 695 rooms. But what makes this architectural marvel stand out to most citizens of Philadelphia is its other world record: the 37-foot-tall, 27-ton bronze statue of the city founder, William Penn. His record? Tallest statue on top of a building.

The Mole Antonelliana in Turin, Italy, was the tallest brick building in the world at a height of 549.5 feet when originally built. However, the tower was rebuilt after a tornado in 1953 destroyed part of it. It now shares second place at 548 feet.

The Gorilla in the Hat

Thanks to an access hatch in Penn's hat, the statute has worn the jerseys of every Philadelphian sporting champion. In 1980, Penn became more than just a sports fan when a man in a gorilla costume stood on the 2-foot-wide brim of Penn's hat to promote the fiftieth birthday of the Philadelphia Zoo's resident, Massa—the world's oldest captive gorilla.

The Second-Tallest Monument in the United States:

Don't Mess with Texas

W hen it comes to big, we've been told to think of Texas. But when it comes to number two, the state speaks for itself. The 567-foot San Jacinto Monument, located on the Houston Ship Channel, commemorates the site in which the decisive battle of the Texas Revolution, the Battle of San Jacinto, took place. For good measure, the octagon shaped obelisk has a 34-foot, 220-ton Lone Star on top. And it's a good thing, too. Without that star, the monument would tumble to number three behind the 555-foot Washington Monument on the list of tallest U.S. monuments.

In a strange twist of Texan logic, the Battle of the Alamo remains much better known than the Battle of San Jacinto, even though the Alamo was a losing battle and the Battle of San Jacinto resulted in the acquisition of nearly one-third of what is now the United States from Mexico.

The Gateway Arch in St. Louis, Missouri, stands 630 feet high and 630 feet wide. This makes it the tallest monument in the United States.

Recuerde San Jacinto!
The Battle of San Jacinto pitted 1,300 Mexican soldiers against the 900-strong Texan army. On April, 21, 1836, the Texans caught the Mexican camp by surprise. With cries of "Remember the Alamo!" and "Remember Goliad!" the eighteen-minute battle resulted in the deaths of 630 Mexican soldiers and 700 prisoners. Only nine Texans lost their lives in the battle. This battle was crucial in the defeat of Mexico and the continued westward expansion of the United States.

Road Warrior

The actual name of that twist of asphalt we call "the interstate" is The Dwight D. Eisenhower National System of Interstate and Defense Highways. Why such a traffic jam of a name? Well, it was named after Eisenhower because he was so instrumental in getting it built. He got his inspiration from serving as the Supreme Commander of the Allied Forces in Europe during World War II. Impressed by how easily it moved troops around in Germany, Ike became an immediate fan of the German *autobahn*.

Connecting Teaneck, New Jersey, to San Francisco, California, I-80 is the second-longest interstate in the United States. At 2,899.54 miles, I-80 trails leader I-90 by a mere 121 miles. Formed in 1956, I-80 beat I-90 by a year. Perhaps, it was quicker to complete because I-80 relied heavily upon existing transcontinental routes from the United States' past such as the Oregon Trail, the California Trail, the First Transcontinental Railroad, and the Lincoln Highway.

I-80 might be second in distance but a 17-mile stretch in southern Wyoming (or, "Snow Chi Minh Trail" in trucker parlance) is among the most deadly motorways in the nation. What makes this stretch so deadly is that it acts as a magnet for some of the strongest winds, slickest ice, and slushiest snow in the country.

From Abe to Ike

The interstate wasn't the first but the second automobile road to traverse the United States. First came The Lincoln Highway; established in 1913, "The Main Street Across America" connected New York's Times Square with Lincoln Park in San Francisco. Eisenhower was a part of the Army's Transcontinental Motor Convoy of 1919 that traveled its entire distance.

Cousins, Cakes, and a Term Cut Short

Only two presidents of the United States were second cousins: James Madison and Zachary Taylor, with Taylor being the second-born of the cousins. Most Americans are probably more familiar with Madison's wife Dolly (at least her cakes, anyway) than they are with the fourth president of the United States, or with the fact that the White House burnt down for the first and only time while Madison was in office.

But to hell with snack cakes and capital destruction, Zachary Taylor was not to be outdone. Nicknamed "Old Rough and Ready" from his bravery during the Black Hawk War, Taylor gained the rank of general and went on to fight in the Mexican War in 1845, from which he emerged as a national hero by defeating the Mexicans. Taylor became just the second president to die in the White House from an illness. Doing so just fifteen months into his office, he became the third-shortest-serving president. He was also the last U.S. president to own slaves while in office.

Sleeping with the Enemy

President Taylor's daughter, Sarah Knox Taylor, married Jefferson Davis—that's right, *the* Jefferson Davis who went on to become the first president of the Confederacy. Shortly after their marriage, the newlyweds headed to Louisiana. It was the second time Sarah visited the state. The first time, she and her two sisters caught malaria—her sisters didn't make it. On her second trip to Louisiana, she (along with her husband) caught malaria for a second time. This time, she didn't make it. Davis went on to take Varina Howell as his second wife.

The Flu Season from Hell

The world was catching its collective breath from the pain and destruction of World War I when a new, global killer struck—influenza. This epidemic was so bad, it went on to become a pandemic. From March 1918 to June 1920, the world caught the flu (in what is known as "the 1918 flu pandemic" or "Spanish Flu") as the virus spread. From the arctic to some of the remotest Pacific islands, few were safe. In total, the influenza epidemic might seem a lowly number two, but don't let its ranking fool you. Once done, it took more lives than those lost in all of World War I.

Most epidemics that have haunted human existence arose out of our health and education conditions of the time. Just as the number one epidemic, the bubonic plague, struck in part due to how well rodents were able to thrive in the squalor of cities, the influenza pandemic of 1918 was made possible largely in part by primitive sanitation conditions and poor public health education. Educating the public on pandemic prevention proved challenging. Not only was it difficult to communicate to many people at once, but many Americans were either illiterate or not fluent in English.

Expect More

In 1918, the average life expectancy for an American was fifty-three years for men and fifty-four for women. Today, men are expected to live to seventy-five and women, eighty. And that's after catching the flu at least once in their life.

The Second Person to Reach the North Pole Overland:

Where's Wally?

When Wally W. Herbert walked across the geographic North Pole in 1969, he was the second person to do so. Or was he the first? Herbert's excursion was documented and undisputed. The same cannot be said about Robert Peary's crossing in 1909. Peary's claim is fraught with so many controversies that many believe he never reached the true North Pole. In fact, it was Herbert who, upon setting out to research Peary's expedition in hopes of eliminating all doubts of his claims, ultimately concluded in his 1989 book, *The Noose of Laurels*, that Peary had missed the North Pole by about 60 miles.

This was oddly fitting for Peary's legacy; he, too, was first considered to have been the second person to touch the top of the world. But when Frederick Cook's claimed crossing proved to be fraudulent, an act of Congress in 1911 declared Peary the first man to have reached the geographic North Pole. Herbert had admired Peary so much that his findings scarred him deeply; while uncovering the truth about Peary's expedition, Herbert suffered three heart attacks. Despite Herbert's findings, the National Geographic Society still recognizes Peary as the first.

A Second Not to Be Forgotten

If you're team Peary, then Matthew Henson is your true second to the Pole. Henson accompanied Peary and wrote a book about his journey as an African-American explorer titled *A Negro Explorer at the North Pole*. Widely ignored for his accomplishments for most of his life, Henson was finally recognized in 1944 with a Congressional medal.

Real American Heroes

The second African American and the first woman to lie in state in the U.S. Capitol was a real American hero, Rosa Parks in 2005. She was named "Mother of the Modern-Day Civil Rights Movement" by Congress. The defining moment in Rosa Parks's life was when she refused to give up her seat in the front of a public transportation bus to a white man on December 1, 1955, in Montgomery, Alabama. The bus driver called the police and Rosa was arrested and charged with a violation of the segregation statute in the Montgomery City Code. This single act of civil disobedience led to the Montgomery Bus Boycott during which African Americans stopped riding public buses. The boycott lasted for 381 days before the statute on public bus segregation was lifted.

Who would you guess was the first African American to be honored by lying in state in the U.S Capitol's Rotunda? The great Dr. Martin Luther King Jr.? Nope. How about Supreme Court Justice, Thurgood Marshall? No, again. The first African American to lie in state was U.S. Capitol Police Officer Jacob Chestnut. An American hero, Chestnut, along with Detective Mike Gibson, was shot to death in an attack on the Capitol in 1998.

Say It Ain't So!

The first player to break the color barrier of Major League Baseball, Jackie Robinson took a similar stand while on a bus. While in the Army at Fort Hood, Texas, Jackie was ordered by an officer to move to the back of the Army's integrated bus, but he refused. The officer recommended that Jackie be court-martialed. Jackie was eventually acquitted of all charges brought against him.

The Second-Tallest President:

Tall Legacies

T he second-tallest president, Lyndon B. Johnson, was just a half an inch shorter than Abraham Lincoln, who takes the title of tallest president. Johnson's first job was a schoolteacher, but he was quick to find a second. He became a U.S. representative, then a U.S. senator, and rose to the position of Democratic majority leader before becoming the vice president of the United States. After John F. Kennedy Jr.'s assassination in 1963, Johnson succeeded him as president. During Johnson's term in office, Congress and President Johnson finished some of the work Abraham Lincoln started with the passage of the Civil Rights Bill of 1964. The Civil Rights Bill prohibited discrimination in employment or use of public facilities. The Voting Rights Act of 1965 protected the rights of black voters and the Civil Rights Act of 1968 forbid discrimination in housing. The Medicare and Medicaid programs were also created during Johnson's term in office. President Johnson appointed the first African American, Thurgood Marshall, to be an Associate Justice of the United States Supreme Court.

Standing 6 feet 4 inches without his hat, Lincoln inches to the title of tallest U.S. president. But it's not for the size of his stature, rather the size of his convictions concerning racial equality for which he is revered today.

LBJ Presidential Library

The Lyndon Baines Johnson Presidential Library is the only Presidential Library that doesn't charge admission. Its attractive admission price might be why it routinely leads all Presidential Libraries in attendance. Lately, the only time it slides to the second spot is during the year or two following the opening of a new Presidential Library.

Give Peace a Second Chance

In October, 1961, a group of 130 volunteers touched down in the Philippines, becoming the second group of Peace Corps volunteers to start their service. These volunteers' initial mission was to work in language, math, and science education. Now, after almost fifty years, nearly 9,000 Peace Corps volunteers have contributed to the ongoing development of the Philippines, but most importantly, they have helped provide a proud face for America and Americans abroad.

Less than a year after he was elected, President Kennedy made good on one of his campaign promises when the first-ever Peace Corps volunteers boarded a plane for Ghana in August 1961. Now, close to fifty years later, nearly 200,000 volunteers have answered Kennedy's call to willingly contribute a part of their lives to serving their country and beyond.

Do You Know What It Means to Miss New Orleans?
On September 7, 2005, in response to the first ever call for the domestic use of Peace Corps volunteers, Peace Corps Director Gaddi H. Vasquez declared: "Over the past forty-four years, Peace Corps volunteers have responded to the needs of humanity worldwide. Today, as many of our fellow Americans are suffering tremendous hardship right here at home, we believe it is imperative to respond. While the Peace Corps is an international volunteer organization, it is incumbent upon us to assist by extending the Peace Corps spirit of giving to our neighbors in the gulf coast region."

The Second White House:

The British Are Coming, Again!

The White House has been called the President's Palace, the President's House, and the Executive Mansion. It wasn't until 1901 that President Theodore Roosevelt officially named it "the White House." The house we know today is actually the second White House. The first one was destroyed when British soldiers set it on fire on August 24, 1814, during the War of 1812. On December 24, 1814, the British and Americans signed a peace treaty to end the war. The president at the time, James Madison, had James Hoban, the original architect of the building, restore the White House.

It took three years to complete the restoration of the new White House. The south and north porticos were later additions in 1824 and 1829 respectively, again by architect Hoban. During his term, President Teddy Roosevelt started a new trend of additions. Since Roosevelt wanted separate spaces for family life and presidential work areas, he turned the third-story attic into livable rooms. The famous Oval Office was added in 1909, and President Truman was in office for the last major renovations—replacing the building's original framework with steel.

What's in a Name?

While it's always been white, the White House's color hasn't always come from paint. Since the White House's stone structure couldn't be painted, its color came instead from the whitewash applied to it to protect the house from the elements. Finally painted white in 1818 with the invention of lead-based paint, the name "the White House" remained a nickname until September 1901, when Theodore Roosevelt made it official.

The Second-Most-Common Element in the Human Body:

It's Not Gas

As far as the rest of the universe goes, carbon comes in as the sixth-most-abundant element. It is also one of the most versatile elements known. Pure carbon can take the three natural allotropic forms: amorphous (e.g., charcoal and soot), diamond, and graphite. Ironically, graphite is one of the softest materials on Earth, and diamond is by far the hardest substance known to humans. With more than 10 million known chemical compounds currently, the number of new carbon compounds will likely increase as more and more new medicines and materials are developed. Adding to its already impressive resumé, carbon is the body's second-most-common element. Carbon atoms are the basis for all proteins, carbohydrates, fats, and nucleic acids.

It might be hard to believe that oxygen is the most common element in the human body because most people think of it as a gas. Most of the oxygen found is combined with hydrogen to form water, making up between 55 percent (for women) to 78 percent (for newborn babies) of the human body.

One Buck of a Discovery

One of the newest discoveries in carbon chemistry is that of the buckminsterfullerene, or buckyballs. Buckyballs are composed of sixty to seventy carbon atoms joined together like a ball. Capable of trapping other atoms inside their framework, these balls have also displayed magnetic and superconductive properties. The 1996 Nobel Prize in Chemistry was awarded to Harold Kroto, Richard Smalley, and Robert Curl for their discovery of buckminsterfullerene.

The Second-Longest Ship Canal in the World:

Thank You Erie Much

You've got to travel all the way to Buffalo, New York, to stand at the start of the second-longest ship canal, the Erie Canal. It has a distance of 363 miles from Buffalo on Lake Erie to Albany on the Hudson River. The Erie Canal, an amazing construction project, was built between 1817 and 1825. The 7-million-dollar project was one of the United States' earliest construction projects.

New York City probably owes the Erie Canal for helping it become what it is today. By establishing direct access with the rest of America's heartland, it was able to transport a growing variety of goods that could not be produced in an urban environment. Some of the benefits of a canal over a roadway for hauling freight are that canal boats can carry more weight than wagons, canals do not become impassable after a heavy rainfall, and they do not ice over in the winter.

The Grand Canal was built in China in A.D. 283 and is still the world's longest shipping canal in the world at 1,114 miles.

What a Ditch

Construction of the canal provided mounds of political fodder. Then-mayor of New York DeWitt Clinton rested so much of his political career upon the project that when the construction encountered setbacks, so did Clinton's career. Before the canal was completed, Clinton was voted out as governor and booted from the Canal Board. Thus, DeWitt became the first, but not last, Clinton to see the words "Clinton's Folly" and "Clinton's Ditch" associated with his political career.

86 The Second Person to Die in the Electric Chair:

Have a Seat

The United States was the first country to use electrocution as a means of ending a criminal's career. Today, there is much debate over the place of such punishment in a "civilized" society. When the electric chair was introduced, however, the most significant debate was where they should plug it in. Two prominent Americans of the time, Thomas Edison and George Westinghouse, were at odds at what type of electric current should be used to power the electricity for the chair, AC or DC.

The second person to be executed by the electric chair was Harris A. Smiler, a convicted murderer, at the notorious Sing Sing Prison, on June 4, 1891. By 1916, Sing Sing had a monopoly on New York's chair-fried humans. The first electric chair execution took place at Auburn Prison in New York on August 6, 1890. William Kemmler was the first person to be executed in the electric chair; his sentence was for killing his lover, Matilda Ziegler, with an axe in a drunken rage. In spite of having had its electric chair unplugged in 1963, New York's 614 electrocutions still leads the nation.

Give Me Your Murderers, Scoundrels, and Pirates, Yearning to Be Executed

Few have heard of Bedloe's Island in New York harbor. But with a history of executing pirates and other ne'er-do-wells, it's got Hollywood horror hit written all over it. Today, Bedloe's Island is better known as Liberty Island, the site of the Statue of Liberty.

Old Ivy

F ounded in 1693 in Williamsburg, Virginia, the second university in America was The College of William and Mary. The college was named in honor of King William III and Mary II who signed the charter for a "perpetual College of Divinity, Philosophy, Languages, and other good Arts and Sciences" to be located in the Virginia Colony. The college was instrumental in the education of America's founding fathers and has been aptly called the "Alma Mater of a Nation." Presidents Thomas Jefferson, John Tyler, and James Monroe all concluded their undergraduate education at William and Mary. The college was the first university to teach law; one of its most notable graduates was Chief Justice of the Supreme Court John Marshall. The position of chancellor of the college has been held by George Washington, John Tyler, Warren Burger, Henry Kissinger, and Sandra Day O'Connor.

Just sixteen years after the Pilgrims landed at Plymouth in 1620, Harvard University began passing out bachelor's degrees in Cambridge, making it the first university in the United States. More than three hundred years later, Harvard's sense of of superiority lives on.

Born-Again Church

Famed British architect Christopher Wren's work on William and Mary's main hall, the Wren Building, wasn't the only architectural impression he left on a U.S. college campus. Halfway across the country, the Church of St. Mary Aldermanbury stands on the campus of Westminster College in Fulton, Missouri. Wren reconstructed the church after the Great Fire of London in 1666 left much of it in ruins. Then, after World War II air raids shredded it for a second time, it was transported brick-by-brick to Westminster College where it was rebuilt according to Wren's original plans.

The Second-Longest-Ruling British Monarchs:

Really, Long Live the Queen

In this battle for power, second place goes to America's favorite king, George III. Since his father died before he could take the crown, George III succeeded the throne from his grandfather, George II, in 1760. George III was a devoted husband to his wife, Charlotte of Mecklinburg-Strelitz, a German princess, who popped out fifteen of his children. Unfortunately, George suffered from a debilitating disease, porphyria. It was so physically debilitating that by the time George got off the throne, he was blind, deaf, and insane. Before that, George lost his power to the prime minister of England thanks to his handling of the American Revolution and his bout with his debilitating disease. Maybe George's biggest mistake was to tax the American colonies to pay for military protection of the British Empire. George brought on more problems with the United States later on when he decided to tussle with them for a second time in the War of 1812.

Queen Victoria won the contest for longest-ruling British monarch with a reign of more than sixty-three years from 1837 to 1901.

A Horse, A Horse! My Kingdom for a Horse!
The third-longest-ruling British monarch is the current queen, Elizabeth II. The eldest daughter of King George VI, Queen Elizabeth took the throne at age twenty-five after her father died in 1952. Elizabeth II is married to Prince Philip, Duke of Edinburgh. They have had four children, eight grandchildren, and countless scandals. The queen loves horses and has a keen interest in and knowledge of horses.

89 The Second City:

Its Citizens Are Second to None

New York is commonly thought of as America's first city because of its incredible population and wealth of opportunities. You only need to go halfway across the country before you reach the country's second city, Chicago, Illinois. A popular belief is that Chicago was branded with the second-city name when *New York* magazine writer, Abbot J. Liegling, used it in the title of his book, *Chicago: The Second City*. Another possible reason for this city's numerical nickname is that, after the Great Fire in 1871 destroyed most of the city, it had to be rebuilt for a second time. The Great Fire proved to be such an important event in the history of the city that some historians use pre- and post-fire Chicago to mark time in their writings.

A couple of areas in which Chicago does not place second to New York: Chicago has fifteen miles of bathing beaches and twenty-six miles of lakefront, while waterfront recreation is sorely lacking in New York. The Art Institutes of Chicago is also famous for one of the largest and most extensive collections of Impressionist and Post-Impressionist paintings. And the Lincoln Park Zoo is one of only three free zoos left in the United States.

Is Chicago Your Kind of Town?

- The Taste of Chicago is the world's largest free outdoor food festival.
- Chicago is the home to the very first blood bank in the United States.
- Chicago claims the world's longest street, Western Avenue, which is lined with more than sixty-two car dealerships along its 23.5 mile length.

The Second Name for Memorial Day:
Decorated, but Not Forgotten

Some Americans might remember their parents and grandparents talking about "Decoration Day" and not knowing what it meant. Decoration Day was the day people would go to the gravesites of loved ones and place flowers on them. The second name for Decoration Day is Memorial Day. General John Logan, the commander-in-chief of the Grand Army of the Republic, felt that the country needed to heal the divide of the Civil War, so he proposed the first Decoration Day. General Logan proposed the date of May 30 for two reasons: many flowers are in bloom in the United States on that day, and it is not the anniversary of any Civil War battle. The first Decoration Day was on May 30, 1868. Nevertheless, Memorial Day was not an official federal holiday until 1971, when Congress created the National Holiday Act that provided for a three-day weekend over the last weekend of May.

The Congressional National Moment of Remembrance

For one minute on Memorial Day, at 3 P.M. local time, Americans are asked to participate in the National Moment of Remembrance. This moment was established by President Clinton in 2000 when he wrote, "In this time of unprecedented success and prosperity throughout our land, I ask that all Americans come together to recognize how fortunate we are to live in freedom and to observe a universal 'National Moment of Remembrance' on each Memorial Day. This memorial observance represents a simple and unifying way to commemorate our history and honor the struggle to protect our freedoms."

The Second Great Fire, on October 8, 1871:

Is It Hot in Here?

What happened on October 8, 1871, that is so historic? Fires broke out in five cities along Lake Michigan's coast. Two days later, thousands of people were dead, and an entire city was almost destroyed. While no one is certain how it started, it is believed that a wind from the southwest blew into Peshtigo, Wisconsin, on October 8. The wind started feeding small fires around town until, all of a sudden, there was an immense rumbling heard across the small town. People ran outside, but all they could see was a bright red horizon. Soon the fire reached the town, where it burned up everything in sight. The embers from the Peshtigo fire crossed into Green Bay before traveling north into Michigan. By the time it died out, 1,875 square miles had burned.

The second great fire occurred later that same night more than 250 miles to the south in Chicago. A fire started in the center of Chicago's office buildings and residences and since everything—homes, buildings, and bridges—was made of wood, the fire had plenty of fuel. In the aftermath, 90,000 were left homeless and 70,000 buildings were totally destroyed, but fortunately only 200 people died.

A Deadly Oversight

Stories about the Great Chicago Fire of 1871 dominated newspaper headlines, but journalists overlooked the most deadly fire in U.S. history, in Peshtigo. Historians believe that between 1,200 and 2,400 people lost their lives in the fire, which swept along the shores of Green Bay. The Peshtigo fire resulted in the greatest loss of life due to a natural disaster in the United States' history.

The Second U.S. President to Be Assassinated:

Thanks for the Advice

Talk about a prize you don't want to win. On July 2, 1881, at a Washington, DC, railway station, James Garfield became the second U.S. president to be assassinated. The assassin was an angry attorney who had been passed over for a government position. Garfield spent weeks in the White House in his mortally wounded condition while doctors tried to find and remove the bullet—with their fingers. Even Alexander Graham Bell tried to find the bullet with one of his new inventions, the induction-balance electrical device. It seemed that President Garfield was recovering, so he was taken to the New Jersey shore for some rest and relaxation, but he died there on September 19, 1881, from an infection, internal bleeding, or one too many fist pumps.

Garfield was the twentieth president of the United States and the last president to have been born in a log cabin. He rose to the rank of major general in the Civil War. It was President Lincoln who encouraged him to resign from the military and run for public office. Garfield took Lincoln's advice and eventually became the "dark horse" candidate for president as a member of the Republican Party, winning the election by only 10,000 votes. Sadly, Abraham Lincoln was himself the first U.S. president to be assassinated in 1865.

More Than You Need to Know about Garfield

- It is believed that using non-sterile instruments and hands looking for the assassin's bullet may have caused blood poisoning that eventually killed him.
- He was the first left-handed president.
- He could speak German and English.
- He was the only president to be an ordained minister.

The Second-Longest Time on the FBI Most Wanted List:

Bad Guys Finish Second

Wanted for armed robbery in 1983 and placed on the list May 14, 1984, Victor Manuel Gerena has been on this list you really don't want to be on for the second-longest time. Gerena robbed his former employer, Wells Fargo, binding and drugging two security guards at gunpoint. Gerena made off with approximately $7 million in the heist and then fled in a rented Buick to Mexico before leaving for Cuba. The FBI suspects that Gerena was recruited by a violent Puerto Rican independence group called *Los Macheteros*. They are believed to have helped smuggle Gerena out of the country. Gerena is considered armed and dangerous, and there is a million-dollar reward for his arrest and conviction.

Donald Eugene Webb, the longest on the list, was placed on the FBI Most Wanted List in 1980. He was never caught, but he has since been removed because he is thought to be dead, thus rendering him significantly less dangerous than Gerena.

Most Wanted Facts

- A minimum reward of $100,000 is offered for information leading to the arrest of a criminal.
- The first woman on the list was Ruth Eisemann-Schier. Seven other women have made the list.
- The oldest person on the list is sixty-nine-year-old James "Whitey" Bulger who is still at large—we think.
- Of the 494 fugitives on the list, 463 have been apprehended. More than 150 of those apprehensions have been made with the public's help.
- The year 2010 marks the sixtieth anniversary of the FBI Most Wanted List.

The Second-Oldest Brewery:

Beer. Don't Leave Home Without It.

Beer has been as much a part of the United States as importing the immigrants to brew it. Much like the Pilgrims and many of its founding fathers, the United States was the second home to many of our founding brewfathers. A German immigrant, David G. Jungling, got the party started in 1829 when he opened his Eagle Brewing. But you probably know it by its second name: Yuengling.

It was a second German, August Schell, who started what is now the second-oldest brewery in the United States after moving to New Ulm, Minnesota, with a group of other Germans in search of a place to carve out a second home that resembled their first. The most important thing missing? Beer. It wasn't long before Schell opened Schell's Brewing Co. in 1860.

Beer Boat

The Pilgrims may have been a little, well, puritanical, in their beliefs, but that didn't keep them from toting enough kegs of beer on their way to the promised land to keep partying like it was 1699. The only problem was that, due to several delays and difficulties getting to the exact location stipulated in their patent with the Virginia Company of London, their supply of beer had reached critically low levels. What were the belt-buckled travelers to do? According to the *Mayflower*'s log: "We could not now take time for further search or consideration, our victuals being much spent, especially our Beere." So rather than sailing a few more degrees latitude south, the Pilgrims pulled over at Plymouth, and the rest is beer-story.

The Last Confederate Standing

Every student of U.S. history knows about General Robert E. Lee, who surrendered his Army of Northern Virginia (20,000–22,000 men) on April 9, 1865, at Appomattox Court House to General Ulysses Grant. However, this did not end the Civil War. On April 26, 1865, General Joseph E. Johnston surrendered his Army of Tennessee and most other active Confederate armies (90,000 men) at Bennett House near Durham Station, North Carolina. This surrender was the second and last major stage in the peacemaking process that brought the Civil War to an end. The president of the Confederacy, Jefferson Davis, did not like the terms of the surrender and ordered General Johnston to leave with his cavalry but Johnston, seeing the futility of the situation, disobeyed the order.

Despite being the second Confederate General to surrender, Johnston was the *first* West Point officer to join the Confederacy (before even Robert E. Lee) and never lost a direct engagement in the war. He was severely wounded at the Battle of Fair Oaks and his command was given to Robert E. Lee.

Thanks a Lot

Once Johnston surrendered his army to General William T. Sherman, the latter, known for his merciless march through Georgia, gave ten days of food rations to the hungry rebel army. Johnston never forgot this act of generosity and even served as a pallbearer at General Sherman's funeral. Johnston contracted pneumonia at the funeral and died a few days later.

The Second Gettysburg Address:

Short and to the Point

In November 1863, the most famous orator and the president of Harvard, Edward Everett, was to deliver the keynote address at the dedication of the national cemetery following the Battle of Gettysburg. Everett spoke for two hours about America's bravery and sacrifice. The second speaker was President Abraham Lincoln. He took a handwritten piece of paper from his coat jacket and spoke. His immortal 272 words only took three minutes to say, and they will be remembered as long as there is a United States.

The *Chicago Tribune* reported that Lincoln's Gettysburg Address would "live among the annals of man," while across town the *Chicago Times* editorial column stated "the silly, flat and dishwatery utterances of the president." Edward Everett wrote "I should be glad, if I could flatter myself that I came as near to the central idea of the occasion, in two hours, as you did in two minutes." Lincoln wrote two copies of the speech before he delivered it and three more copies after the speech for charitable purposes. Only one copy, dated March 1864, has Lincoln's signature on it.

Honestly, Wrap It Up Already

The absolute irony of the two speeches is that Lincoln's Gettysburg Address was one of his shortest speeches ever. While he was campaigning for president, it wasn't unusual for Lincoln's speeches to last two or even three hours. However, he was able to keep the attention of his audience no matter how long he spoke.

Lady Lindy

The second person to make the solo flight across the Atlantic was also a first. Aviator Amelia Earhart was not only the second *person*, she was also the first woman to make the long, lonely flight. But her resemblance to Air Chuck didn't end with her aviation abilities and daring. Amelia had such a close physical resemblance to Charles Lindbergh that she was called "Lady Lindy." But this was not her first transatlantic flight. Amelia was brave enough to go as a passenger when Wilmer and Louis Gordon made their flight. Sadly, most people know her only as "the woman who went missing" on her record flight around the world at the equator. Amelia's solo flight across the Atlantic began on May 21, 1932, exactly five years to the day of the Lindbergh flight. She took off from Harbour Grace, Newfoundland, in a Lockheed Vega airplane and touched down in a field near Londonderry, Northern Ireland, after a fifteen-hour flight. For the flight, Congress awarded Earhart the Air Force Distinguished Flying Cross; she was the first woman to receive the award. In August 1932, Amelia became the first woman to fly solo nonstop coast to coast across the United States.

The first person to fly solo across the Atlantic Ocean, in his Spirit of St. Louis, was Charles "Lucky Lindy" Lindbergh.

Early Earhart
Amelia realized that she wanted to fly early, when she was seven years old. Her father, Edwin, took her to the 1904 St. Louis World's Fair where she rode a Ferris wheel for the first time. During the ride, she discovered she was not afraid of heights.

Just Hanging Around

Built in 2680 B.C., the Pyramids of Egypt are considered the first wonder of the ancient world. The second wonder is the Hanging Gardens of Babylon, which were supposedly constructed by King Nebuchadnezzar II for his queen, Amuhia, about 600 B.C. But some accounts attribute the building of the gardens to Nebuchadnezzar's homesick wife—daughter of the King of the Medes—rather than King Nebby II. Their marriage was arranged to create a peaceful alliance between the two nations. However, Amuhia's homeland was green and mountainous, whereas Babylon was a depressingly flat, barren, and sun-baked land. The king created the Hanging Gardens to look like a mountain with lush vegetation growing on it. The Hanging Gardens are believed to have been 400 feet long, 400 feet wide, and anywhere from 80 to 320 feet high.

One of the most challenging parts of the gardens wasn't its construction but rather getting water to its plants in the hot, dry desert from the Euphrates River. A water chain was devised in which two pulleys connected by a chain of water buckets were used to bring water to the top of the gardens. Archeologists are not 100 percent certain that the Hanging Gardens really existed because there is no mention of it in Babylonian literature—only in Greek references.

So, That's Why . . .
The Babylonians had a number system with a base of sixty. Consequently, they divided the days into the same time periods we use today: twenty-four hours of sixty minutes and sixty seconds in each minute.

The Second Rameses of Egypt:

The Ladies' Man of Egypt

Rameses II was the grandson of Rameses I, the first king of the nineteenth dynasty, and was called Rameses the Great. Rameses I only ruled for a couple of years and wasn't half the stud his grandson was. Rameses II had more than 200 wives and concubines, who gave him ninety-six sons and sixty daughters in his ninety-six years of life. He outlived many of his sons, and his thirteenth son was crowned king upon Rameses II's death. Rameses II had a mighty army and greatly expanded the Egyptian territory, but he seemed to be more interested in constructing buildings and monuments. One such example is the temple of Amon-re at Karnak, with its columned great hall. Rameses II also finished the monument his father started at Luxor and Karnak. His most famous structure, though, was the temple at Abu Simbel, with its four carved figures in the sandstone cliffs. Rameses II was buried in the famed Valley of the Kings. His tomb was 8,800 square feet—the largest of all ancient Egyptian tombs. He wasn't only a skilled builder but also an expert planner. The construction of his tomb started in the second year of his reign. The mummy of Rameses II is one of the best preserved. His kingdom would go on to survive for almost 150 years after his death.

Abu Simbel Moving Day
In the 1960s, Egypt was building the Aswan High Dam, but it would have submerged the temple of Abu Simbel in its reservoir, so the government disassembled the temple and moved it on to a cliff, 200 feet above the original spot where it was reassembled.

An Impeach of a President

The second president to be impeached wins first place for juiciest impeachment to date. Bill Clinton was impeached on charges of perjury and obstruction of justice on December 19, 1998, by a vote of 228 to 206 of the House of Representatives. Independent Counsel Kenneth Starr led the charge with an inquiry into several allegations aimed at the president, including a sexual harassment suit. During the inquiry, Starr received audiotapes in which a former White House intern Monica Lewinsky said that she had a sexual encounter with President Clinton. Clinton denied this under oath, and Lewinsky produced her Clinton-stained dress. Clinton then admitted his involvement. After a twenty-one-day hearing, the U.S. Senate acquitted Clinton on the perjury charge by a vote of 55 to 45. The obstruction of justice charge vote was split 50-50.

The first U.S. president to be impeached was Andrew Johnson on February 24, 1868, by the House of Representative's vote of 126 to 47. Johnson dismissed Secretary of War Edwin Stanton without the permission of Congress, thus violating the Tenure of Office Act. Johnson was acquitted by the U.S. Senate by only one vote.

The Cost of Defection

The Johnson impeachment hinged on one vote by Kansas Senator Edwin Ross. Ross voted against removing Lincoln from office. As a result, Ross was rejected and near poverty at the end of his life. John F. Kennedy Jr. stated that Ross rose above passions and partisan politics and "may well have preserved for ourselves and posterity constitutional government in the United States."

God is Holy and Jealous

The first commandment the Big Guy gave Moses on Mount Sinai was "Thou shalt have no other gods before me." The second commandment was "Thou shalt not make unto thee any graven image, or any likeness of anything that is in heaven above, or that is in the earth beneath, or that is in the water under the earth: thou shalt not bow down thyself to them, nor serve them: for I the Lord thy God am a jealous God, visiting the iniquity of the fathers upon the children to the third and the fourth generation of those who hate Me, but showing steadfast love to thousands of those who love Me and keep My commandments." Exodus 20:1–6.

As you can see, the second commandment is a bit more detailed than the first. It clearly states God's expectations, as well as that God gets jealous and that there are negative and positive consequences to one's actions. When Jesus was asked by the Pharisees "What is the most important commandment?" Jesus replied: "Thou shalt love the Lord thy God with all thy heart, and with all thy soul, and with all thy mind. This is the first and great commandment. And the second is unto it, thou shalt love thy neighbor as thyself. On these two commandments hang all the law and the prophets."—Matthew 22:37–40

Who Wrote Exodus?
Moses is believed to be the author of the first five books of the Bible: Genesis, Exodus, Leviticus, Numbers, and Deuteronomy, which are known as the Pentateuch.

What's the Answer?

Few people actually know the second verse of our National Anthem, which answers the question posed at the end of the first verse: "Oh say, Does that Star-Spangled Banner yet wave over the land of the free and the home of the brave?" Apparently not known for being short-winded, Francis Scott Key answered with:

> *On the shore, dimly seen through the mists of the deep,*
> *Where the foe's haughty host in dread silence reposes,*
> *What is that which the breeze, o'er the towering steep,*
> *As it fitfully blows, half conceals, half discloses?*
> *Now it catches the gleam of the morning's first beam,*
> *In full glory reflected now shines in the stream:*
> *'Tis the star-spangled banner, O! long may it wave*
> *O'er the land of the free and the home of the brave.*

Key was aboard a British ship trying to win the release of an American doctor when the British opened fire on Fort McHenry near Baltimore on the night of September 13, 1814. Key and his doctor friend could see the American flag flying over the fort as the rockets lit up the sky. At dawn of the next morning, they looked at the fort and they saw the war-torn U.S. flag still flying over the fort.

A Second-Spangled Title

Key first wrote a four-stanza poem titled "The Defence of Fort McHenry" describing the bombardment of Fort McHenry, which was changed to the Star-Spangled Banner. It became the official national anthem by an act of Congress in 1931.

The Second Voyage of Columbus:

In 1493, Columbus Sailed the Ocean . . . for a Second Time

I n 1492, Christopher Columbus made his first voyage to the New World with three ships and 100 men. Columbus's second voyage in 1493 was a major undertaking with seventeen ships and over 1,000 men for a colonization project. For the first time, domesticated animals like pigs, horses, and cattle were brought along on this voyage. Columbus was to set up a trading post, try to find gold, and continue to search for China and Japan.

The second voyage was the fastest, taking only twenty-one days. Columbus left thirty-nine men behind on his first voyage because one of his ships wrecked, but he discovered that all the men had been killed as punishment for raping some of the indigenous women. Columbus went on to spend five months establishing the settlement of Isabella on the northern coast of Hispaniola and exploring the rest of the island. The Spanish Crown appointed Columbus as governor, but he was a very poor administrator, and the colonists soon hated him. The second voyage was the beginning of colonialism in America, and Spain was on its way to building a mighty empire in the coming years all based on the gold and silver it found in the New World.

Notable People on the Second Voyage
Columbus's brother Diego was on the second voyage, and Columbus left him in charge of the settlement when he went back to Spain. The Spanish explorer, Juan Ponce de Leon, first became the governor of Puerto Rico and journeyed to Florida seeking the Fountain of Youth.

PART 3

Runners Up in the World of Science and Technology

How many times have you said to yourself, *on second thought, this or that might be a better way of doing things?* For scientists, second thoughts and second attempts are as common as lab coats and absentmindedness. Scientists often first create prototypes of objects to see if they can accomplish the tasks they were designed to do. After the first few trials, if the prototype survives, the scientists might experience a "eureka moment" or go back to the drawing board. Regardless, they learn from their firsts so they can achieve with their seconds. In the world of science and technology, firsts get things started, but seconds keep the world moving forward.

The Second-Tallest Habitable Building in the United States:

Whatchu Jalkin' 'Bout, Willis Jower?

C hicago is home to the two tallest habitable buildings in the United States. Right down the street from the top dog is the second-tallest habitable building, the ninety-two-story, 1,362-foot-tall Trump International Hotel and Tower. It was completed in 2009 at a cost of $847,000,000.

The Trump Tower Chicago, as the locals call it, went through three designs before beginning construction. The first design was a building that was rather short and wide, the second design was too boxy, but the final design had curves and resembled a ship sailing though a sea of skyscrapers. The Trump Tower also pays homage to the Art Deco skyscrapers that have made Chicago such a great, architectural metropolis. When the building was completed, it held the record of being North America's largest reinforced concrete building. Its concrete construction allows for more window space and less sway than a steel building. Reportedly, The Donald has bought the $28 million, eighty-ninth-floor penthouse.

The tallest habitable building in the States, the Willis Tower (formerly Sears Tower) is 110 stories and stands at 1,451 feet tall.

The Third Empire

The Empire State Building has gone from the tallest habitable building in the world to the fifteenth, but it will always be the first to have 100 floors. Since 1978, runners have raced up 1,576 of its steps to the eighty-sixth floor. The record time was set in 2003 by Paul Crake with a time of nine minutes and thirty-three seconds. The second place time of nine minutes and thirty-seven seconds is shared by Crake (2001) and Darrin Eisman (1994).

The Rusty Arches

Welcome to Fayette County's "Bridge Day" Festival. For the past thirty-one years, on the third Saturday in October, people from all over the United States descend on the New River Gorge Bridge close to Fayetteville, West Virginia. Traffic is stopped on the bridge in order to allow for demonstrations of BASE jumping, repelling, and ascending the 876 feet of the bridge base. Bungee jumping has been prohibited from Bridge Day since 1993, because it's the BASE jumping that spectators come to see.

West Virginia's largest, one-day festival is the only day it is legal to jump from the bridge. The spectacular steel-arch bridge is the second-highest vehicular arch bridge in the world, just behind the 1,125-foot-high Millau Viaduct in France. The New River Gorge Bridge held the record for the longest arch bridge with the length of 1,700 feet until recently, when two longer bridges were built in China in 2003 and 2009. The bridge has a rust-like exterior that never needs painting due to the Cor-ten steel used in its construction.

New River Gorge Facts

- West Virginians call "Bridge Day" the largest extreme sports event in the entire world. BASE jumpers by the hundreds converge from around the world to legally jump from the New River Gorge Bridge.
- Over 1 million visitors come to the New River Gorge National River each year.
- The Royal Gorge Bridge in Colorado is higher than the New River Gorge Bridge, but it's a suspension bridge.

The Second-Longest Galaxy:
Great Walls and Blobs of the Cosmos

For the average Joe with a working knowledge of the universe, it can be tough to think beyond the usual galactic shapes of spirals, ellipticals, and other irregular shapes. Maybe, you've even heard of superclusters, where many individual galaxies are in close proximity to each other. Within these superclusters, some galaxies even collide with other galaxies. Astronomers have discovered networks that appear to be filaments linking galaxies together that stream along for millions of light-years. The second-longest galactic filament is the Pisces-Cetus Supercluster with an estimated length of 1 billion light-years and width of 150 million light-years. This supercluster spans about one-tenth of the known universe, and the clusters have around 1,000 galaxies in each one. Astronomers have found gigantic blobs of gas interspersed within these superclusters called Lyman apha-blobs (LABs). Some of these blobs are more than 400,000 light-years across—making them four times the size of our Milky Way galaxy.

At this point in time, the largest galactic filament is the Sloan Great Wall, discovered in 2003 by J. Richard Gott III and Mario Juric of Princeton University. The filament is 1.37 billion light-years long and about 1 billion light-years from Earth.

Your Space Address
The Milky Way has between 200 and 400 billion stars; our sun is merely one of them. Nearly 80 percent of all galaxies are a part of a supercluster. The supercluster to which we belong is Virgo Supercluster. So if you were to give your address for an intergalactic package, it might look something like this:

- (Your Name)
- Earth
- Milky Way Galaxy
- Virgo Supercluster, Pisces-Cetus Supercluster Complex

The Flowers of the Cosmos?

Nebulae are considered "flowers of the cosmos" because of their many shapes and colors. Technically, they are giant clouds of gas and dust either lit from within or backlit from very bright stars.

The Carina Nebula (aka NBC3372, or the Great Nebula in Carina) is the second-largest nebula. In its boundaries are two of the most luminous and massive stars, Eta Carinae and HD 93129A in our galaxy. Carina Nebula is not as famous as the Orion Nebula, but it is brighter and four times larger. Maybe, this is because it is located in the constellation, Carina, which is in the sky over the southern hemisphere. The nebula is about 100 light-years across and is estimated to be 9,000 light-years from the Earth. The nebula is an incubator for about twelve "infant" stars being produced there.

Short-Lived Super Star

Eta Carinae is probably the most extraordinary blue variable star in the Milky Way. It illuminates with 4 million times the power of our sun, yet it is only 100 times larger than our sun. There are only about twelve stars out of the billions in the Milky Way that reach that strength and size. Stars that size are getting close to the Eddington Limit: the point where the outward force of the nuclear reaction is stronger than the inward pull of gravity. In 1843, Eta Carinae went ballistic, producing a near supernova explosion that made it the second-brightest star for a few years.

Where Was the First Bungee Jump?

In the island country Vanuatu, where bungee-jumping is called *naghol*, or land diving, men have been jumping from wooden towers with vines wrapped around their ankles (instead of elastic cords) for centuries. Today, the world's highest bungee spot is the Macau Tower in China, with a distance of 1,109 feet.

The second-highest site is the Royal Gorge Bridge in Canon City, Colorado, with a height of 1,053 feet. Part of the thrill of the Royal Gorge Bridge is walking on it. Its floor is made of 1,292 wooden planks with scenic views of the Arkansas River below. Adding an element of adventure to walking across it, wind easily sways the bridge back and forth. Most who cross it (let alone, jump off of it) consider the Royal Gorge Bridge one of the scariest in the world. At 1,260 feet long and only 18 feet wide, it is able to support over two million pounds. Construction of the bridge began in June of 1929 and was completed just six months later without a single fatality, incident, or bungee jump.

Grab Your Grass Skirts and Penis Sheaves

During *naghol*, men remove their western clothes and grab their penis sheaves, while women don their finest grass skirts. This 75-foot headfirst dive is a rite of passage for young men as well as men of all ages who seek to impress a grass-skirted girl, to settle a village dispute, or apparently, just to see whose sheaf is bigger. *Usually* no one gets killed by the dive, but internal organs—particularly spleens—are not always so lucky.

The Second Man to Circumnavigate the Earth in a Balloon:

Up, Up, and Away...and Away

T he second person to circumnavigate the globe not only did it in less time than the first guy—he did it alone. Steve Fossett took off in his ten-story high balloon, the Spirit of Freedom, from Northam, Western Australia, before landing it back in Australia just fourteen days, nineteen hours, and thirty-three minutes later. During this historic "second," Fossett also set the record for the top speed of a balloon flight with an amazing 186 miles per hour. Along with setting the world's fastest speed and fastest time around the world, Fossett also claimed two more records: the longest-distance solo flight in a balloon (20,602 miles) and, on July 1, 2002, the longest twenty-four-hour distance (3,186.8 miles) traveled in a single day. Fossett had made five previous attempts to fly around the world before his successful sixth attempt. It took Bertrand Piccard and Brian Jones fewer than twenty days in 1999 to make the first nonstop balloon trip around the world. The 28,432-mile flight is considered aviation's longest in time and distance.

A Speed Blimp

While an airship can be steered from the inside, a balloon relies on outside winds to guide it. In addition to holding the record for the fastest balloon flight in 2004, Steve Fossett also holds the record for the fastest flight (71.5 mph) in an airship. He did it aboard the Zeppelin NT. During his life, Fossett set over 100 world records, sixty of which were still standing by the time of his ill-fated, final flight on September 3, 2007.

Big Ol' Jet Airliners

The Airbus A380 is the largest passenger jet plane, with almost twice the floor space of the second largest, the Boeing 747. But with a top speed of 604 miles per hour, it's the Boeing 747 that flies to the top as the fastest passenger jet in the sky.

How many parts does it take to get the second-largest plane off the ground? Six million. Out of those six million, more than half of them are some type of fastener. Pretty odd, considering a single roll of duct tape could probably do the job. Perhaps, it's tougher to hold together than it is to get off the ground.

The 747's first flight was February 9, 1969. The latest figures for the fleet are 42 billion nautical miles, which would be the equivalent of 101,500 trips to the moon and back. More than 3.5 billion passengers—over half of the world's population—have flown on a 747.

The Spruce Goose Is Not So Spruce.
The world's largest flying boat, the Spruce Goose, is made of wood; but it's made of birch, not spruce. One more misnomer: the plane isn't a goose either. Its real name is the H-4 Hercules. This Goose made its one and only flight on November 2, 1947. It lifted 70 feet above the water, reached a top speed of 135 miles per hour, and traveled about 1 mile. While the Goose may not have broken aviation records for speed or distance, it still holds the record of being the world's largest wooden airplane.

The Second-Largest Bone in the Human Body:

A Shank Stronger Than Steel

Pound for pound, human bone is stronger than steel. Bone has the tensile strength of about 20,000 pounds per square inch (psi); regular steel's tensile strength is 70,000 psi, but steel is four-and-a-half times heavier than bone. Do the math: bone wins the strength contest easily. Bones are even eight times stronger than concrete.

The *second*-longest bone (behind the femur, or thigh bone) is one of the two leg bones located below the knee, called the *tibia*. But you might know it as your *shinbone* or, the ever-popular *shank bone*. When it comes to length, the tibia might come in second, but when it comes to strength, the ole shank bone makes no bones about which bone is the strongest in the body. Your shinbones better have some strength. After all, they support most of your body's weight. The same can't be said about the other bone in the lower leg, the *fibula*. Rather than being relied upon for support, the fibula acts more as a stabilizer for the tibia, keeping it in alignment with the knee and ankle. Not all tibias are created equal: in males, the tibia is vertical and parallel with the fibula; in females, the bone is still vertical, but more slanted.

Bone Up on Bone Facts

- Babies have more bones at birth than adults.
- Half of the body's bones are located in the hands and feet.
- The smallest bone in the body is the stirrup, which is located in the inner ear and is no bigger than half the size of a grain of rice.

The Second-Brightest Dwarf Planet and Plutoid:

From Pluto to Plutoid

Astronomers are constantly searching for new names for objects that do not fit the regular scheme of things. Dwarf planets and plutoids are almost the same things, just with different names. Simply put, plutoids are trans-Neptunian dwarf planets, or large orbiting objects outside Neptune that have enough gravity to give them the greatest amount of gravitational pull in their vicinities. The brightest of these dwarf planets is one that most people know by name, Pluto. Many planet fanatics were very disappointed when Pluto was demoted from a "real" planet to a dwarf planet.

The second-brightest plutoid is Makemake, or the plutoid formerly known as 136472, 2005 FY9. So what makes Makemake so special? Makemake has the distinction of being the fourth-identified dwarf planet and the third-identified plutoid. Makemake's apparent magnitude of about 16.7 is so bright that it can be seen with some amateur telescopes. In 2009, there were only four plutoids: Pluto, Eris, Haumea, and Makemake, with more than seventy objects waiting to see if they will make the list.

Crazy Cosmic Lexicon

A plutino has a particular attraction to Neptune and no other planet. A plutino orbits the sun twice, while Neptune obits three times around. Cubewanos are objects in close proximity to plutinos but not influenced by Neptune's gravitational pull. As we get closer to Earth, space is filled with flying NEOs (Near-Earth Objects). These flying rocks are objects that cross Earth's orbit and have the potential to slam into Earth. Lastly come the dreaded PHAs (Potentially Hazardous Asteroids).

Dips, Craters, and Bears, Oh My!

Callisto, the second-largest moon of Jupiter, is named after the nymph Callisto of Greek mythology. Outsized by only two moons in our solar system—Jupiter's Ganymede and Saturn's Titan—Callisto leads our solar system in one category: most cratered object. Callisto has two huge impact craters that look like giant bull's-eyes, which have been named Valhalla and Asgard. Valhalla is considered to be the largest-impact crater anywhere in our solar system. Callisto's surface is made of dirty ice, and it is thought to have a subterranean, salty ocean.

It's fitting that Callisto's craters look like bull's-eyes because the nymph after whom it was named was the target of her first born son, Arcas. Transformed into a bear by a jealous Hera, Arcas came across his mother in bear-form. When she ran to give him a bear hug, a frightened Arcas fired. Before his arrow hit its mark, Zeus took pity on them both, whisking them up into the night's sky as *Ursa Major* and *Ursa Minor*—Latin for Big Bear and Little Bear, but more commonly referred to today as the Big Dipper and Little Dipper.

Moontel Callisto?

Callisto might be the best hope for some intergalactic shut-eye in the near future; it is considered to be the best site for a human base for the exploration of the Jupiter system, according to a 2003 NASA Human Outer Planets Exploration (HOPE) study. Callisto's low radiation from Jupiter and its stable geology also make it a potential location for refueling. NASA believes that a manned flight to Callisto could happen as soon as the 2040s.

The Second-Largest Gland in the Human Body:

Twice as Nice

The largest gland is the liver, and it happens to be the second-largest organ. The second-largest gland is located near the liver; it's the pancreas. This "hidden" gland lies deep within the body, hidden behind the stomach. The pancreas is shaped like a fish, with one end larger than the other, and is only about 6 to 8 inches long and about 1½ inches wide.

On the underside of the pancreas, tiny tubes carrying digestive enzymes come together like the veins of a tree leaf. Your pancreas produces digestive enzymes that play a major role in breaking down the proteins, carbohydrates, and fats in food so they can be absorbed by the body. The pancreas has within it groups of tissue called the islets of Langerhans, which manufacture all the important hormones insulin, glucagon, and somatostatin. The beta cells produce insulin, which decreases the amount of sugar (glucose) in the blood. Meanwhile, the alpha cells produce glucagon, which increases the amount of glucose, and the delta cells make somatostatin, which controls the cells that make insulin and glucagon.

Pancreatic Facts

- Insulin comes from the Latin word for island, *insula*.
- Only 2 percent of the pancreas is composed of islets of Langerhans.
- A restaurant sugar packet could hold all the blood sugar you have in your body.

Second-Largest Planet in the Solar System:

A Planet Floating on Water

Our solar system's second-largest planet, Saturn, is the least dense planet. If it were placed in an ocean of water, it would float. In spite of possibly having a solid inner core, it is made mostly of gas. Even though it is not as large as Jupiter, it has those incredible rings that make it probably the most recognizable of all the planets. Jupiter, Neptune, and Uranus have rings, but they are neither as visible nor striking as Saturn's, which do not touch the planet but orbit high above Saturn's equator at the same angle. There are seven major rings that contain thin ringlets numbered in the thousands. These ringlets are composed of billions of ice particles that range in size from dust specks to chunks more than 10 feet across. While Galileo Galilei first discovered Saturn's rings in the early 1600s, it wasn't until 1980 that the separate ringlets were discovered.

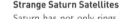

Strange Saturn Satellites

Saturn has not only rings but also has twenty-five satellites. The largest, Titan, is larger than both Mercury and Pluto. Titan is one of the few satellites that has an atmosphere. Titan is just the first of Saturn's strange satellites: Mimas has a crater one-third its size; the contrast between Iapetus's light and dark sides is so great, its light side reflects ten times more light than its dark side; and Hyperion is one of the largest, non-spherical objects in our solar system. In fact, this cylindrical satellite is the second largest non-spherical satellite in the solar system after Neptune's Proteus.

Second-Largest Moon:

A Home Away from Home?

In 2005, the Huygens probe landed on the surface of Titan, the second-largest moon in our solar system, to collect data from its surface. The Huygens probe hitched a seven-year ride along a Cassini-Hygens spacecraft before hopping off for a parachute landing on Titan. This mighty moon bears many incredible similarities to Earth. It has constant bodies of surface liquid and a full, thick, layered atmosphere. The details of this moon have been a mystery, thanks to a permanent haze that hides the surface from telescopes and spacecraft. Evidence indicates that Titan has a climate in which it rains methane and ethane gases instead of water and wind. Titan has many lakes; one is about as large as Lake Superior. Sand dunes and shorelines are seen and change during the seasonal storms. One strike against investing in Titan's shoreline real estate: its surface temperature is -290 degrees Fahrenheit. Titan is also the only planetary body other than our moon, Mars, and Venus on which humans have landed a spacecraft and taken images of its surface.

What Is a Cryovolcano?

According to Rosaly Lopes, a radar scientist at the Jet Propulsion Laboratory, "If Mount Vesuvius had been a cryovolcano, its lava would have frozen the residents of Pompeii." Cryovolcanos were first witnessed on Neptune's moon, Triton, in 1989 by Voyager 2. Scientists have now even seen evidence of cryovolano activity on Titan. Instead of hot molten rocky magma, leaving the vent, the cryovolcano spews liquid water, methane, and/or ammonia. These ejections immediately freeze due to the extremely low atmospheric temperatures, making cryovolcanoes the universe's coolest volcanoes.

The Second-Largest Star:

Failing Heavyweights of the Universe

The good news is that red supergiant stars are the largest in the universe. The bad news is that they're dying. When giant stars enter the last stages of their lives, they swell up to enormous, supergiant sizes. The largest is considered to be VY Canis Majoris, which has an estimated radius 2,000 times that of our sun. The second largest is thought to be WOH G64, which has almost the same radius. If a star the size of WHO G64 were in our solar system, it would extend to Saturn.

What sets WOH G64 apart from a super star like Canis Majoris is that WOH G64 exists well beyond our Milky Way Galaxy. You'd have to set your course to the Large Magellanic Cloud Galaxy to witness WOH G64. Compared to the relatively close Canis Majoris, just 5,000 light-years away, WOH G64 is a whopping 160,000 light-years away. Oh, and good luck trying to spot it with your telescope from the United States—it can only be spotted from the southern hemisphere.

What Can Spot a Tennis Ball 300 Miles Away?

The Very Large Telescope Interferometer in Chile can. Astronomers use two giant telescopes to "see" the heat signature of stars and compute accurate images of them. Even with their enormous size, the world's largest optical telescopes have had a hard time observing the dark matter that surrounds stars in the Milky Way Galaxy, let alone neighboring galaxies.

Would You Cross A Bridge Taller Than the Eiffel Tower?

What about two that size? The two tallest bridges in the world are both more than 1,100 feet tall. The second tallest is Millau Viaduct reaching a height of 1,125 feet. This Viaduct traverses over the Tarn Rive in southern France with a road deck of 890 feet. The roadway is 8,070 feet long (that is longer than the Champs-Elysees) and 105 feet wide. One of the most amazing engineering feats was the placement of the roadbed on the pylons. The entire road was slid out from both sides across temporary and permanent pylons. Gigantic hydraulic rams were employed to push the 40,000 tons of roadway at a snail's pace of 2 feet every 4 minutes. The roadbed is made of steel, which is much lighter than most bridge roadbeds made of concrete. The construction of the bridge was started in December 2001 and completed in December 2004. The bridge was built to shorten the distance from Paris to the southern coast of France.

Rocket Bridge

The tallest bridge at 1,837 feet tall is still being built in China; the Siduhe Grand Bridge is slated to be finished in 2012. The Siduhe Grand Bridge will span a distance of 3,200 feet. One major problem posed by its construction was getting the steel cables from one side of the valley to the other side. The engineers used a novel approach but an old technology developed by the Chinese: the rocket. The engineers attached the steel cables to rockets and shot them across the valley.

The Second-Fastest Train:

Speed Rails

Unlike the first in this category, the second-fastest train in the world is the French TGV, and it uses good, old-fashioned metal rails and electric-powered train wheels. The TGV beat its own speed record in April 2007 by reaching a speed of 357.18 miles per hour. To accomplish this, though, the train was modified with larger wheels and fewer cars.

The TGV serves about 200 cities in France and the normal operating speed is between 174 and 186 miles per hour. For several years, the TGV held the record for the fastest scheduled train rides, with an average speed of 173.6 miles per hour from start to stop. This record was recently beaten in 2009 by the Chinese Wuhan-Guangzhou High-Speed Railway. The Wuhan-Guangzhou holds the record for the fastest scheduled train ride with an average speed of 217 miles per hour, even though it has not reached the fastest (or second fastest) top speed for a train.

The world's fastest train moves 361 miles per hour, but not on tracks or rails. Instead, it glides along a cushion of air. The Japanese JR-Maglev uses a magnetic-levitation track in which very strong electromagnets lift the train a few millimeters off the track and, by switching the polarity of the magnets, fire the train forward.

Puff, the Magic Dragon!
Apparently, it doesn't take much to slow down the Wuhan-Guangzhou. It was stopped by an object less than three inches long—a cigarette. A smoking passenger activated a switch that caused the train to stop for a two-and-a-half-hour delay. The train could have completed its 700-mile journey in the same time as the impromptu smoke break.

Channel + *Tunnel* = *Number Two*

Connecting Honshu and Hokkaido islands, Japan's 33.46-mile Seikan Tunnel is the world's longest rail tunnel. Only fourteen miles of the tunnel are under the seabed, but it goes 460 feet beneath the seabed, 790 feet lower than sea level. Even though it's the longest, it's proven to be the most useless. It is quicker and cheaper to fly from the islands than it is to ride through the tunnel; Seikan isn't just underwater, it's underutilized.

The second-longest rail tunnel is the Channel Tunnel. The Channel Tunnel, or Chunnel, connects Great Britain with France and holds the record for the longest *undersea* tunnel in the world with a distance of 23.5 miles. The Chunnel is recognized as one of the Seven Wonders of the Modern World by the American Society of Civil Engineers. The Chunnel carries more than 16 million passengers a year. The Chunnel's tunnel has two railways 98 feet apart for the trains to travel. Trains exceed 100 miles per hour and take only twenty minutes to get through the Chunnel.

Competitive Chunnel

The two machines that drilled through the rock to create the Chunnel were twice the size of a football field and could chew up to 250 feet of rock a day—and it still took three years to finish. One of the machines started on the English side of the Channel, and the other began on the French side. British and French tunnel workers had a competition to see which team could get to the center first. The British won.

The Second-Fastest Production Car:

Speed Will Cost Ya!

What's the sticker price on the world's fastest production car, the Barabus TKR? It'll set you back a half-a-million bucks while pulling you forward at 270 miles per hour. The second-fastest production car is named after the French racing driver Pierre Veyron, who won the 1939 Le Mans. The Bugatti EB Veyron has just four fewer horses than the Barabus and comes within 20 miles per hour of its top speed—but, with a $1.5 million sticker price, costs about three times as much. The Bugatti EB Veyron has 1,001 horsepower and an 8-liter, quad-turbo W16 engine. That's right, *W*16, not *V*16. A W16 is an engine in which two V8 engines have been joined together to make a W configuration. The Bugatti held the speed record so long that people still think it's still the champ. It's no wonder, because the car has some memorable specs: it goes from zero to 60 mph in 2.5 seconds and can go from 60 miles per hour back down to zero in a whisper over 2 seconds. The Bugatti also claims the title of "Car of the Decade" by *Top Gear*.

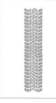

Got Some Good News and Some Bad News for You

Everyone hates flat tires, but Bugattis take them to a whole new level. Replacing a set of tires for your Bugatti will set you back about $25,000. But that's just the start of your expenses. The tires can only be removed in France, and the service to replace them runs $70,000. The good news is that you shouldn't have to wait long to have it looked at: only 200 Bugattis have been sold since 2005.

Dinos in Space!

No, it isn't the title of Hollywood's next Dwayne Johnson movie vehicle—it actually happened. In 1998, the second-fastest dinosaur ever to roam the Earth hitched a ride on the Space Shuttle Endeavor. Actually, it was only the skull of a *Coelophysis* that shot over 18,000 miles per hour through space to the MIR space station to be used in experiments on the effects of microgravity. Coincidentally, the *Coelophysis* was not only the second-fastest dinosaur on Earth; it was also the second dinosaur to travel to space. The first? The *Maiasaura*. The thin air of space must have taken its toll on both of these dinosaurs, though. Both made questionable career moves: the *Coelophysis* starring as Spot in the 1974 television classic *Land of the Lost* and the *Maiasaura* making a cameo in an episode of *Go, Diego, Go!*

The *Gallimimus*, with estimated speeds of 35 miles per hour, is thought to have been the fastest dinosaur on Earth. The *Coelophysis* is believed to have traveled roughly 25 miles per hour. Since the highly sophisticated Seiko stopwatches we have today weren't around during the age of dinosaurs, these are just estimates.

Prehistoric Stopwatch
How do scientists calculate a dinosaur's speed? They examine evidence, both inside and out. First, they measure fossilized trackways to get an idea of how far apart the dinosaurs' feet were when they moved. Then, like C.S.I. investigators, they scrutinize the shape and structure of the dinosaur: bipedal (walking on two feet), bird-like dinosaurs with hollow bones (for a lighter body), and long, slim hind legs have all of the ingredients for swifter movements than their clunkier cousins.

The Second-Largest Organ in the Human Body:

It's Got You Covered

The largest organ in the human body is also the most commonly seen. Despite claims to the contrary, your *skin* is your largest organ. The skin of an adult male can weigh 8 pounds and cover 22 square feet. The liver is your second-largest organ, with a weight of 3 pounds. But when it comes to glands, the liver has no equal. It easily breaks the pancreas down to the body's second-largest gland.

Your liver is not only your second-largest organ—it's also your friend. For starters, if your liver is healthy, it can filter 540 gallons of blood every day. But that's just for starters. Your liver does over 500 different chemical functions. It's a combination of a manufacturing plant, a recycling center, and a waste disposal site. All the food and most of the drugs you take will pass through your liver. It detoxifies any poisonous substances you might have ingested and removes toxic chemicals in the air you breathe. The liver is also your storehouse for sugar, vitamins, and minerals—especially iron. The manufacturing part of your liver builds clotting agents, bile for digestion, and new proteins.

Amazing Regeneration Ability

No other organ can regenerate like the liver. With as little as 25 percent of its own, living tissue, it can regenerate back to its original size. This is a concern with liver transplants because doctors wouldn't want a transplanted liver to outgrow its new owner. A normal liver can regenerate in one to two months; damaged livers can take three to five months.

Gordo, but Not Forgotten

As Smithsonian.com's Robin T. Reid puts it: "The Soviet astronaut who was the first man in space actually was the second upright hominid to make the jaunt. First place went to a thirty-seven-and-a-half-pound, well-tempered chimpanzee named HAM." That Soviet was Yuri Gagarin. Less than a month later, American Alan Shepard became the second human in space.

With the launch of a few fruit flies (they survived the flight) into space in 1941, Americans officially launched the animal space race. The Soviets countered in 1957 by launching a husky (as in dog) named Laika into orbit. Not only was she the first animal to orbit the Earth, but she was also the first to suffer an orbital death. In their rush for "firsts" in their space race with the United States, the Soviets skimped on a re-entry plan; this game of fetch was not meant to be finished.

A year after Laika's orbit, America launched Gordo, a squirrel monkey, into orbit. The United States even hooked Gordo up with a re-entry flight plan. Tragically, Gordo's parachute didn't open. After a short search, Gordo was declared lost at sea. Now he's remembered as the second animal to orbit Earth.

Monkey See, Monkey Do

There must be a shortage of dogs and monkeys in Iran because in 2010, the country launched a rat, two turtles, and some worms into space. Maybe, Iran is just caught up with its firsts. According to President Mahmoud Ahmadinejad: "If last year was our first presence in space, this year is our living creatures' first presence in space. This is a sign of bigger achievements to come."

125 The Second-Largest Producer of Coal in the World:

Mine Your Own Business

The largest producer of coal in the world is China. China has more than 10,000 coal mines and a million miners. The United States is the second-largest producer of coal with an annual output of 1.1 billion tons—20 percent of the world's coal supply. If the United States uses coal at the same rate as today, its coal reserves should last another 245 years. Most people think that West Virginia or Pennsylvania is the top coal-producing state, but that title goes to Wyoming. The cowboy state produced 400 million tons in 2004. However, the neighboring state of Montana has the most coal reserves with 119 billion tons. The state that *consumes* the most coal is Texas, which uses around 100 million tons a year. If you break down the yearly per capita coal usage, it would be 3.8 tons for every person in the United States. Most of the coal (9 out of every 10 tons) in the United States is used in making electricity (it's the cheapest way of producing electricity). The U.S. coal reserves have more potential energy than the entire world's known oil reserves. Nearly 9 percent of all U.S. coal is exported to Japan, Western Europe, and other countries—even China.

Why Keep Canaries in Coal Mines?
Coal miners have long had a soft spot for canaries, but not for their singing. Canaries are more sensitive to the deadly methane and carbon monoxide gases that can build up in mines than humans. If the canaries were singing, everything was cool; but if the canaries croaked, it was time to climb out.

Apple Bytes

If you can remember the 1970s and 1980s, you probably remember Apple Computers, and the first Apple you remember is probably number two.

The second Apple computer was the Apple II, launched in 1977 with several improvements. It had a plastic case and could display color graphics on its screen. Due to the lack of funds to mass produce the Apple II, Steven Wozniak and Steve Jobs offered it to Commodore Business Machines, but Commodore was not interested (Commodore declared bankruptcy in 1994). The cost of the Apple II with two game paddles and a demonstration tape was one of the most reasonably priced personal computers of the day at $1,298. A disc drive was later added in 1978, and it remained unchanged until 1980. About six million Apple II series were sold before they stopped production in 1993.

Wozniak and Jobs debuted the Apple I in April 1976 for $666.66, but few took it seriously. It consisted of little more than a printed circuit-board—you had to buy a tape-interface separately and build your own case.

An Apple Day

On May 24, 2010, Microsoft achieved a notable second. According to the *New York Times*, that was the date Microsoft became the number two most valuable technology company in the world. Why no celebration? Because it was a demotion—Apple was responsible for taking over the top spot. Thanks to the success of its new iPad—more than 2 million sold since April, 2010—Apple seems to have plugged into a new era of technological leadership.

Freedom Power

Nuclear power has been harnessed to generate tremendous amounts of electricity. Since they need to keep that Eiffel Tower lit, it makes sense that the country with the second most nuclear reactors is France, with fifty-nine. As a matter of fact, the French nuclear reactors generate about 77 percent of all the country's electricity. The only other country close to that amount is Lithuania, with 64 percent of its electricity coming from nuclear power. The United States, the country that started the nuclear revolution, with all of its 104 reactors only produces 19 percent of its total electric power with them. The French company Areva is one of the leading builders of advanced nuclear power plants in the world. Currently, Areva is building its first Generation III nuclear reactor. France has the reputation of being the world's largest exporter of electricity to nearby countries. It's exporting about 15 percent of its nuclear generated electricity, which adds about 3 billion euros ($3.6 billion) to its economy. It also exports its nuclear reactors, fuel products, and services to South Korea, South Africa, and China, to name a few. The French also enjoy the cleanest air in the industrialized world and have fewer CO_2 emissions because of its nuclear power generation.

New, Clear Energy

The number of operational nuclear reactors stands at 439 in thirty-one countries with forty-one new reactors under construction. The United States is the leading producer of nuclear energy in the world. Why nuclear power? Aside from the occasional Silkwood shower, nuclear power is much safer, more efficient, and more powerful than other types of energy.

The Cell Continent of India

C hina leads the world in both cellphone production and use. According to the CIA's *World Factbook 2008*, China had 649,700,000 cellphone subscribers. The country calling the second most on their cells is not the United States, but the country to which most of our calls are currently directed: India. According to the same book, India has 376,120,000 subscribers waiting to take your call. India has only about 38 million landlines in the entire country, which means that there are 13 cellphones for every landline phone. More than 20 million telephone subscriptions are being added each month with most being cellphones. The urban centers are almost 100 percent saturated with subscribers, while the rural areas are approaching 20 percent saturation. Due to advances in technology, it is more economical to place cellphone towers around large countries like India and China than to string telephone wires for telephone operations to individual homes.

I Just Called to Say, You Lose

The first mobile phone was a 1960 Swedish car phone, but it probably needed a truck to haul its 80+ pounds around. This "mobile" phone could also drain a car battery in just six calls! The second mobile phone was the winner of a 1973 phone race between Motorola and Bell Labs. How was the winner of the race determined? Dr. Martin Cooper at Motorola used his mobile phone to call Dr. Joel S. Engel at Bell Labs to let him know. It would be another ten years before the Federal Communications Commission would approve the first commercially available mobile phone: Motorola's $3,995 DynaTAC.

129

The Second Nobel Prize Awarded to a Woman:

Second Science Success

The 1903 Nobel Prize in Physics was divided among Henri Becquerel, Pierre Curie, and his wife, Marie Curie. Becquerel was awarded for his discovery of spontaneous radioactivity, and the Curies were awarded for their research on the radiation phenomena discovered by Becquerel. Marie Curie was awarded her second Nobel Prize in 1911 in the field of chemistry for discovering the radioactive elements radium and polonium (named for her native country, Poland).

Critics were quick to question whether or not she deserved her prize in chemistry, as they claimed her research was similar to that of her earlier prize in physics. Some went as far as to suggest she was given the award in sympathy because her husband, Pierre, had been hit by a horse-drawn wagon and killed in 1906. Knowledgeable chemists of the time, though, concluded the discovery of radium and subsequent isolation of a small sample of radium to be the greatest event in chemistry since the discovery of oxygen. Her discovery was the first proof that an element could be transmuted (changed) into another element—a discovery that would revolutionize the future of chemistry.

It Must Run in the Family

Marie and Pierre's daughter, Irène Joliot-Curie, didn't fall far from the chemis-tree. She was awarded the 1935 Nobel Prize in Chemistry, sharing it with her husband, Frédéric Joliot (apparently, sharing Nobel Prizes also runs in the family), for their discovery of the artificial production of radioactive elements. With her award, Irène put the Curies in first place when it comes to total Nobel Prizes per family. But stay tuned: the Kardashians are hot on their trail.

Science in Their DNA

In 1897, J. J. Thompson made history when he discovered the double helix subatomic particle, the electron. It was the first major scientific discovery at the renowned Cambridge University in London, England.

The second major discovery made at Cambridge University came in 1953, when two researchers, James D. Watson, a biologist from Indiana University, and Francis Crick, a physicist, discovered the double helix structure of the DNA molecule. Watson and Crick were helped by the collaboration of several top scientists. Rosalind Franklin, a thirty-year-old English chemist who made an X-ray crystallographic picture of the DNA molecule, was a key player in their discovery. Linus Pauling, the Nobel laureate who had recently discovered the helical nature of some proteins, was also a major contributor. The work of Erwin Chargaff, a biochemist, helped bring a greater understanding of the configuration of the DNA molecule. Maurice Wilkins, a New Zealand physicist, also contributed X-ray photos of the DNA molecule. The discovery of the DNA structure is thought to be the most significant event in biology in the past 100 years.

Forgotten Fourth

The team of Watson, Crick, and Wilkins received the 1962 Nobel Prize for Medicine for their work on the structure of DNA. But they couldn't have done it without Rosalind Franklin. Unfortunately, Rosalind Franklin died of ovarian cancer in 1958. It's believed that her cancer may have been caused by her work with X-rays and other kinds of radiation. Since the Nobel Prize has never been awarded posthumously, we'll never know if Rosalind Franklin would have received a share of the prize.

The Second-Most-Common Human Blood Cell:

Go on Red

White blood cells (WBCs), called leukocytes, are the second-most-common cells. WBCs are the body's police system. They detect and hunt down pathogens (such as bacteria and viruses) and non-living foreign bodies. They perform an amazing service to the body in spite of only making up about 1 percent of the blood in a normal adult. Neutrophils are the cells responsible for finding and destroying bacteria and fungi in the body. Even though the lives of neutrophils are not long (from six hours to a few days), they're filled with purpose. During their brief existence, they gobble up deadly pathogens. Leukocytes are constantly being replaced by the bone marrow every minute. In fact, millions of leukocytes are made each minute of every day.

The liquid part of the blood is called plasma; it's a light, straw-colored yellow, rather than a ravishing red. Blood contains solid cells that can be separated using a centrifuge (a machine that uses gravity to separate materials by spinning rapidly). The most common human blood cell is the red blood cell. Red blood cells (RBCs) are responsible for carrying oxygen and removing carbon dioxide.

The War on Pathogens

Lymphocytes are one amazing type of cell. Memory T cells remember the structure of harmful pathogens and alert the body to an invasion of germs. Once invaded, cytotoxic T cells engage in chemical warfare to destroy the bad guys. None of these two would work without the incredible helper T cell that uses chemical markers to tag the evildoers so other white blood cells can do their job in eliminating them.

The Brightest of the Bright

Even those unfamiliar with *Harry Potter* and Howard Stern have probably heard of or seen Sirius, the "dog star." It's hard not to see Sirius, since it's the brightest star in the sky. The name Sirius comes from the Greek word meaning "scorching" or "searing" because in early times it began to appear in the sky during the hottest part of the Greek summer.

The second-brightest star is Canopus. As far as brightness goes, Sirius has a definite advantage over Canopus. At only 8.5 light-years away, Sirius is the fifth-closest star to our sun. Canopus, on the other hand, is 316 light-years away and is categorized as a yellow-white F supergiant with an average surface temperature of 12,000 degrees Fahrenheit. Canopus is sixty-five times larger than our sun and 14,800 times more luminous. If you are in its visible zone, Canopus can be easy to spot. It's the brightest star on the horizon, just below Sirius, the brightest star in the sky. People in the southern hemisphere can easily see the two brightest stars, Sirius and Canopus, in the sky from their vantage point; from this perspective, Canopus and Sirius look like bright twin stars.

Canopus Facts

- During the 1800s, Canopus was bumped out of second place when Eta Carinae went ballistic, creating a light brighter than Canopus for a brief period before cooling off again.
- Canopus is famous for its use in space navigation. Several spacecraft use the "Canopus Star Tracker" camera to keep on track when traveling through space.

133 The Second-Most-Valuable Traded Metallic Element:

Rare and Pricey

Imagine paying $4,700 for 3.5 ounces of anything. That's what platinum, the second-most-valuable traded metallic element, goes for. Platinum is so rare that all of it ever mined would fit in the size of a living room. Thanks to the catalytic converters in automobiles, the need for rhodium and platinum has increased. Platinum acts as a catalyst to complete the combustion of unburned hydrocarbons in the exhaust of car engines. We've also heard rumors that platinum is very valuable to the jewelry industry where it is made into rings and other fine pieces of female Viagra. And there's a reason Mr. T's necklace is made of gold: platinum is not just more valuable than gold, it's heavier.

Someday, platinum might even save your life; many medical and laboratory instruments are made from platinum because it does not corrode and is an excellent conductor of electricity. It's also the only metal used in the pacemaker's electrodes placed in the heart. Many of the most effective chemotherapeutic agents used in the treatment of cancer use platinum-containing compounds as well.

Rhodium, the most valuable metallic element, goes for $13,000 for 3.5 ounces (the weight of a Willy Wonka Exceptionals Scrumdiddlyumptious Milk Chocolate Bar) of metal. We'd prefer the chocolate, thank you very much.

Going, Going, Gold
The third-most-valuable traded element is everyone's favorite, gold. A one-foot square cube of solid gold weighs a ton...literally. But you better get some before it's gone. According to the Gold Council, 65 percent of all the gold in the world has been mined since 1950.

134 The Second Commercially Formatted Videotape:

May the Best Cassette Lose

The Sony Corporation fired the first shot in the home videotape cassette recording war with its Betamax cassette format in 1975. The JVC subsidiary Matsushita launched the second commercial videotape cassette format, the VHS, just one year later, and the race was on to see which one would win the competition for the public's dollars. Since the two formats required different players and cassettes (not unlike the recent battle between HD DVD and Blue-ray) consumers had to make a choice.

In truth, the Betamax cassette was technically superior to the VHS cassette. The Beta cassette was more compact and efficient, but it had a fatal flaw: it could only hold an hour of content. On the other hand, the VHS tape could hold two hours, which allowed consumers to record an entire movie while the family was away. In spite of the superior sound and picture quality of a Betamax, those qualities could not win out against the overall convenience of a VHS tape. Hollywood also proved to favor the VHS format for their movies.

Wanna Watch My Laserdisc?
Just as the Beta/VHS saga was starting up, a third party threw its format in the ring. In 1978, the first laserdiscs slid into shelves across the nation where most of them would remain undisturbed until the laserdisc was obliterated from the scene when the all-digital DVD format was launched. Although technologically superior to tapes, they cost more and frequent flipping of the discs made them frustrating to play.

135 The Second-Tallest Habitable Building in the World:

Free Nosebleeds

The second-tallest habitable building, rising 1,470 feet, is the Taipei 101 in Taipei, Taiwan. Did you know that Taipei isn't just a city? It's also a mnemonic device. It stands for Technology, Art, Innovation, People, Environment, and Identity. The 101 symbolizes the idea of striving for beyond perfection—not just total size. The Taipei 101 has two of the world's fastest elevators, which have a top speed of 3,314 feet a minute. At that rate, you can make it to the top floor in less than thirty seconds. Since the Taipei 101 is in an earthquake prone zone, a 900-ton tuned mass damper was placed on the eighty-seventh floor to counteract the force of an earthquake or typhoon. Tragically, a 6.8 earthquake stuck before the damper was in place, knocking down two cranes and killing five construction workers during construction. The Taipei 101 was formally opened on New Year's Eve 2004.

The tallest habitable building in the world is the Burj Dubai, in Dubai, United Arab Emirates, at a height of 2,684 feet.

The "Hole" Building
The third-highest habitable building in the world is the Shanghai World Financial Center in Shanghai, China. The Center does have one world record, the tallest habitable building with a hole in it. Its trapezoidal hole was the second choice for its designers. Their first choice was a round hole, but the Chinese thought that it looked too much like the rising sun on the Japanese flag.

136 The Second-Most-Abundant Element in the Universe:

It a Gas, Gas, Gas!

Out of all the ninety-two natural elements the second-most-abundant is helium, which is also the second-lightest element (the first in both categories is hydrogen). Helium is found in the stars along with hydrogen, but on Earth helium has to be hidden or it would leave the planet. Just take a look at any helium filled balloon. What happens? It goes up because helium is lighter than all of the other gases in the Earth's atmosphere. If left alone, the balloon would continue to rise until it reached the top of Earth's atmosphere, much like releasing a piece of Styrofoam at the bottom of a swimming pool.

So, where do people get their helium to fill up balloons and talk like chipmunks? Helium is trapped in deposits underground. Much of the world's helium supply comes from oil wells. At the top of underground oil reservoirs is natural gas—or methane gas—trapped inside the gas is the lighter helium gas. Helium is a product of radioactive decay and is also found in ores of uranium and radium. Helium remains as a gas when all other gases turn into a liquid or solid at absolute zero. Only when extra pressure is applied to helium will it liquefy.

Helium Madness
Ever inhale helium to talk funny? Don't. This practice is potentially dangerous because oxygen deprivation could occur and asphyxiation would follow. Another fun way to kill yourself (or get on the news) with helium: it takes about 160,000 helium-filled balloons to lift a 200-pound person in the air. Start your calculations.

137 The Second American to Patent Barbed Wire:

The Devil's Rope, A Dork's Tattoo

It's been said that barbed wire influenced the United States' westward expansion and way of life as much as the rifle, telegraph, windmill, and locomotive in the 1800s. Jacob Haish was the first to get a patent for barbed wire, but he didn't try to promote it or put it on the market. The second American to patent the "devil's rope," in 1874, was Joseph Farwell Glidden, who was known as the "Father of Barbed Wire." Ouch! Glidden used an improvised coffee grinder to make the barbs for his barbed wire. Glidden found a business partner, Isaac Ellwood, his local hardware store owner. As it so happened, Ellwood had been an unsuccessful barbed wire maker. In 1874, the business, the Barb Fence Company, manufactured 10,000 pounds of the barbed wire; by 1875, more than 600,000 pounds of the sharp fencing was hitting the market. Glidden's barbed wire design also started a creative revolution in barbed wire that would go on to produce over 570 barbed wire patents. However, Glidden's barbed wire was less expensive to erect than the other kinds, thus making his more widely used.

The Barbed Wire Museum
LaCrosse, Kansas, is home to the Kansas Barbed Wire Collectors Association Swap and Sell, held the first weekend in May. Over 2,000 barbed wire collectors and enthusiasts attend the meet each year. The Barbed Wire Museum in LaCrosse has the most unusual specimens of barbed wire, including a raven's nest made entirely of barbed wire.

PART 4

Natural Deuces

Most of us have heard or used the term "second nature" to describe people. In the natural world, second natures don't exist—living things must rely solely upon their innate, instinctive behavior. Having the time and ability to develop a "second nature" is a luxury only humans enjoy.

One thing is for sure: you can't control nature. Mother Nature has her own rules and ways of existing with or without the human need to judge or evaluate it. Nature isn't concerned about rankings or ratings systems. Instead, every aspect of nature contributes its own, small part to the totality of the natural world. Humans call the lion "the king of the jungle" just because it's at the top of its food chain; yet, if the prey and plants lions feed on were to vanish, the lion would be the next to vanish. As we interact with the natural world around us, why not try to appreciate *everything* nature has to offer? Who knows what second impressions your second glances might reveal!

Whippet Good

Welcome to the wide world of whippet racing. Sure, it might sound like a dangerous, new fad among today's teens, but whippets are dogs, and racing is what they are born to do. In fact, whippets are the second-fastest dogs on the planet. The fastest dogs in their weight category, these graceful creatures can reach speeds of 30 to 40 miles per hour. In terms of all dogs, only the greyhound is faster, clocking speeds of 45 miles per hour—but the greyhound is also a much heavier, more muscular dog.

The whippet came to be known as the "poor man's racehorse" because many lower-class, nineteenth-century Englishmen bet on whippet races. Both greyhounds and whippets are sight-hounds who hunt their prey over large open areas at high speeds. Unlike many dogs that use their noses to follow the scent of their prey, these dogs key in on the quick movements of their prey and chase after it, using their eyes to guide them.

Recession Hound

Bigger is not always better, and the whippet owes its existence to people's belief in such an axiom. The whippet breed was developed by mating greyhounds with other breeds of dogs in the hopes of creating a miniature greyhound. Why? Cause this ain't our first recession. Smaller dogs equaled easier boarding and less food—two of the primary factors influencing a racing dog's profit margin.

139 The Second-Deepest Canyon:

Sure, It's Grand

The deepest canyon cutting the Earth is Yarlung Tsangpo in China with a depth of 19,715 feet. The second- and third-deepest canyons are in Peru: Colca Canyon (11,488 feet) and Cotahusasi Canyon (11,001 feet). The Grand Canyon is only about half as deep as Colca Canyon. But the Colca Canyon's walls aren't as steep as the Grand Canyon's. Colca is Spanish for the small holes found in the cliffs of the canyon. It's believed that the Incas and pre-Incas used these for food storage. But it's also thought that some were used as tombs for significant people. Colca Canyon has gone through many names: The Lost Valley of the Incas, The Valley of Wonders, and The Territory of the Condor are just a few of the names it has had before finally settling on Colca. The canyon is also one of the few places the elusive Andean Condor can still be spotted.

Hide-and-Go-Seek Champion of the Mid-fifteenth Century
In 1995, a 500-year-old ice mummy named Juanita was found on one of the Colca Canyon volcanoes when its eruption melted the snows that had hidden her frozen body. While scientists were elated about her discovery, they weren't necessarily surprised. Juanita wasn't their first ice mummy. About forty years earlier, the Mummy of El Plomo Peak was the first frozen, high altitude, Inca human-sacrifice mummy ever discovered. Juanita became the second.

140

The Second-Fastest Dolphin:
Who's Responsible for Dolphin-Safe Tuna?

With an estimated population of 3 million, the Pacific Spotted Dolphin is second to the bottlenose dolphin as the most abundant on the planet. It's also the second fastest. Only the Dall porpoise can beat its 17 mile-per-hour swim. Sure, this porpoise has been clocked at speeds of 35 miles per hour, but what have they done for the dolphin community as a whole? The Pacific Spotted Dolphins, on the other hand, offer so much more than speed. First of all, they're extremely playful animals. They like to swim aside boats, skip across the water, perform acrobatic tricks, and jump out of the water. Their jumping out of water helps fishermen spot tuna that swim along with the dolphins. For some unknown reason, the Pacific Spotted Dolphins like to swim with yellowfin tuna, even though the dolphins have no interest in eating the tuna. This dolphin behavior (along with the use of purse seine nets) is estimated to have contributed to deaths of about 4 million dolphins. But public outcry over the deaths of so many dolphins has helped change some of these methods, resulting in dolphin-safe tuna.

Dolphin Speed Limits
Ouch! Researchers in Israel have discovered that swimming produces microscopic bubbles around the animal's tail. When these bubbles collapse, they produce a shock wave. Dolphins have nerve endings located in their tails, so it hurts more when the shockwave hits. Fast swimming fish like the tuna don't have nerve endings in their tail so they don't feel the pain, even though pits from the shockwaves form on their tails.

*It's a Bird... It's a Plane...
It's—No, It's Just a Bird*

Just a bird? Peregrine falcons reach speeds comparable to today's fastest racecars. Diving down on their prey, they top out at 200 miles per hour. But these dive-bombers must rely heavily on gravity to assist them in reaching their maximum velocities. The spine-tailed swift, the world's second-fastest flier, on the other hand, cruises at 106 miles per hour, but they do so in horizontal flight, relying only on the flapping of their wings. They belong to the needle-tailed swift group because their tail feathers converge into a single point unlike most swifts, which have a forked tail. Regardless of what you call it, this swift must really like to fly because it seldom lands on the ground voluntarily. Instead, they spend most of their time in the air, catching insects. So attuned to living up in the air, these birds can even drink water while flying. For the longest time, many Australians believed that the swifts didn't land until they finally observed a couple of them in trees.

Pickup Dives

It may not have the most masculine name, but the Anna's hummingbird males are as macho as they come when they want female birds to notice them. Male Anna's hummingbirds incorporate high-speed diving as a part of their elaborate courtship rituals designed to raise their cool quotient with the ladies. Females had better have eyes like a hawk, because these guys can really hum during their dives, and they can reach speeds of 385 times their own body length per second!

What's the Only Animal with Feet on Its Arms?

It's the sea star, but known by many as a *starfish*. How heavy can it get? Coming in second at a hefty 11 pounds is the ever popular sunflower sea star. And this second-place star is a winner when it comes to speed. They've been clocked moving at 10 feet a minute! The *Thromidia catalai*, which lives off the coast of New Caladonis in the South Pacific, can reach 13 pounds, but no word on how fast that stocky star can move.

Even though they begin their lives with the sea star standard five arms, sunflower stars grow an additional nineteen arms, thus providing the reasoning behind their name. Only the second heaviest, the sunflower is thought to be the largest. Some can achieve an amazing arm span of more than 39 inches. They also have the incredible ability to disjoint some parts of their body. Sunflower sea stars might have the appearance of a rainbow, but they've got the appetite of Kobayashi. Unlike many other sea stars, this sunflower can even swallow an entire, muno-esque, sea urchin . . . mmm, gabba, gabba.

Twist, Bite, Slide, and Vault: The Stop, Drop, and Roll of Sea Star Safety
The sunflower sea star is a rapacious predator. But its prey have a few tricks up their shells. When captured, snails will twirl around to free themselves. Red and purple sea urchins use their pedicellariae (pinchers) to bite at the sea star's grasping arms. The California sea cucumber remains as cool as a cucumber and slides away. The cockle is the most creative: it lowers its strong foot and pole-vaults to safety.

Vegetative Healing

W hen we think of the largest living creatures on Earth, blue whales typically come to mind. However, the two largest living organisms aren't animals. In fact, the second-largest organism in the world is a group of trees connected by a common root system. The second-largest living organism on Earth is a 105-acre colony of Aspen trees in Utah, called Pando (Latin for "I spread"). Even though Pando is made up of several trees, the trees are all genetically identical. Technically, this makes these trees of the Pando clones of its original tree. Weighing in at an estimated 6,615 tons, Pando is second to none when it comes to being the heaviest organism on the planet. With an age believed to be somewhere between 80,000 and a million years old, it's also one of the oldest living organisms on Earth.

How's all of this possible? Go watch *Avatar*. Similarly to the Na'vi, Aspens are one of the many plants that reproduce vegetatively rather than sexually. This means they send out roots horizontally—sometimes up to 100 feet away—to sprout up into new tree clones. This works well against forest fires because new trees easily pop up after fires since their roots are protected underground.

A Humongous Fungus Among Us
Oh, and the *largest* organism? It's an underground fungus in Oregon, known as the Humongous Fungus, and it has expanded to over 2,200 acres. Another example of the power of vegetative reproduction, *Armillaria gallica* (Humonguous's scientific name) started as nothing more than a microscopic spore sometime between 2,000 and 8,500 years ago.

Volcanoes Gone Wild!

As far as the second-largest undersea volcano goes, it's a bit of a tossup. Scientists do believe, however, that over 75 percent of all volcanic eruptions taking place this very minute are doing so under the ocean. Since undersea volcanoes, or seamounts, can grow with each eruption, it's hard to tell which one is the largest at any given time.

Two seamounts are candidates for the title of second-largest underwater erupter. The Marsili seamount, situated between Sicily and Italy, is one. It's also very active—and feared. One of its eruptions could create a tsunami strong enough to hit the Italian coast. The Loihi Seamount is the other. Twenty-five miles off the coast of the Big Island, Hawaii, it's the most recent volcano produced by seamount hotspot Hawaii. Even though it's more than 10,000 feet above the ocean floor, it has another 3,199 feet to go before it reaches the ocean's surface and can become Hawaii's newest island—something it is believed to do in the next 10,000 to 100,000 years. In 1996, Loihi stirred, creating swarms of over 4,000 recorded earthquakes in a two-week period. The largest undersea volcano spurs far less debate: it's 15,000 feet tall, 30 miles across at its base, lies off the coast of Sumatra, and has yet to be named.

Deep Lava

Imagine the sight of 2,500 degrees Fahrenheit lava hitting near freezing seawater. In December 2009, an ocean research ship launched a remote-controlled submersible, *Jason*, to study the volcanic eruption of the Pacific Ocean's West Malta volcano. West Malta is 6 miles long, 4 miles wide, and ascends 1 mile from the ocean floor. Despite this size, its summit still lies 4,000 feet under the surface of the ocean.

The Second-Fastest Fish:

What's 14 Feet Long, Travels 60 Miles per Hour, and Weighs Almost a Ton?

The Atlantic blue marlin. With its curves like the hull of a racing yacht, the Atlantic blue marlin obviously resides in the Atlantic Ocean, but other types of marlins populate the Pacific and Indian Oceans as well.

Even though its 60 miles per hour is fast, the blue marlin is only the second-fastest fish in the ocean; the fastest is the Indo-Pacific Sailfish. This sailor has been clocked at speeds of 68 miles per hour— only 2 miles per hour slower than a cheetah. What makes it faster than the blue marlin? Size might be a place to start. Weighing in at 220 pounds, the speedier Indo-Pacific Sailfish is four-and-a-half times lighter than a female blue marlin. That's right: female. Female blue marlins can weigh three times more than male marlins. But both sexes swing a mighty spear. The blue marlin's spear is not for show; it uses it to slash back and forth as it travels through schools of fish. The marlin then goes back and feasts on all of the stunned and injured fish floating around.

Old Men and Their Fish

In Ernest Hemingway's *The Old Man and the Sea*, poor Santiago pursues an Atlantic blue marlin. While his intense struggles leave him with plenty to contemplate but little to eat, his outcome also accurately reflects today's reality: most marlin fishers end each day empty-handed. The difference, though, is that they do so thanks to their practice of catch and release rather than ravenous sharks. If it makes modern man that much less existential, then so be it.

Big and Yucky

Almost all bacteria measure just 0.5 to 5.0 micrometers (1 micrometer is 1/1000th of a millimeter). With the exception of viruses, bacteria are the tiniest cellular organisms; they are so small that millions are released every time we sneeze. Tens of millions are found in every gram of soil or milliliter of river water. Without a doubt, they're the most abundant living things on our planet. They have adapted to live in places no other organisms can: from the hottest geyser springs to the coldest, darkest ocean depths.

The largest known bacterium was discovered off the coast of Namibia in a smelly, sea floor ooze. It was named *Thiomargarita namibiensis* and measured up 0.75 millimeters wide. It could be seen without a microscope. The second-largest bacterium, *Epulopiscium fishelsoni*, was found in the intestine of a marine surgeonfish species and measured 0.7 millimeters which is still 150 times larger than the typical bacterium. By the way, the largest human cell is the human egg cell, which is about 0.1 millimeters (the size of the point of a pin).

Super-Sized Bacteria

What's puzzled scientists the most about extremely large bacteria cells is how they transport nutrients and energy throughout their large, cellular masses. During a 2002 scientific investigation of the *Epulopiscium fishelsoni* bacterium, Esther Angert of Cornell University discovered an amazing peculiarity. She determined that bacteria have large amounts of DNA distributed evenly throughout their cells. This allows for a more efficient protein synthesis.

What Did the Megafish Say When It Hit a Concrete Wall? DAM!

One of the largest concerns to megafish (freshwater fish that measure longer than six feet or exceed 200 pounds) populations and health is the building of dams. The Three Gorges Dam in China is having a negative impact on the Chinese paddlefish, which some biologists believe is the largest freshwater fish. Unfortunately, this size-king may already be extinct. The last time one was sighted was in January 2003. The largest North American freshwater fish, the white sturgeon, has failed to reproduce since the Libby Dam was completed in Montana in 1974, stopping essential nutrients from flowing to their spawning beds.

How does one determine the largest fish? Is it the longest fish or the heaviest? The Chinese paddlefish is 23 feet long and can weigh 1,100 pounds. The white sturgeon can grow to 15 feet and tip the scales at a whopping 1,500 pounds. Take your pick as to which one you think is the largest and the second largest. In case it might influence your choice, the white sturgeon has very unusual scales; they're made of bony plates instead of the standard fish scales.

The Great White Hope

The best news for the white sturgeon is a Kootenai Indian tribe's hatchery. The hatchery has thousands of year-old sturgeons that were the offspring of two wild, adult sturgeons. It has released over 80,000 juvenile sturgeons into the river. However, no one will know the success of the project for at least thirty years because it takes sturgeons that long to reach sexual maturity.

Polar Versus Kodiak: Which Bear Is Bigger?

Did you guess the Polar bear? Then, you're partly right. Did you guess the Kodiak bear? Then, you're also partly right. That's because there's barely any difference in size among the males. So, that makes the *female* Polar and Kodiak bears the second-largest land carnivores.

Male bears of both species can reach a standing height of 8 to 11 feet and weigh between 500 and 1,000 pounds. The females can stand 8 feet tall and weigh between 400 and 700 pounds. Kodiak bears only live on the Kodiak Archipelago islands in Alaska. Their current population is around 3,500 bears, which translates to 0.7 bears for every square mile.

The Polar bear's scientific name is *Ursa maritimus*. For all you non-Latin-speaking nerds, that means the "ocean bear." Fitting, since it spends more time in the ocean on a chuck of sea ice than on land. The Kodiak has its quirks as well. Technically, the Kodiak bear is an omnivore because it feasts more on plants, berries, and fish than on baby seals. In fact, it spends very little time hunting down other mammals to eat.

Hibernating Astronauts
NASA is fascinated by the fact that bears can hibernate for more than eight months a year. During this time they don't eat, drink, or eliminate wastes; yet, they experience very little bone mass loss and no muscle tone depletion or blood poisoning from nitrogen wastes. Knowing the secrets to these incredible abilities could help astronauts during extremely long space voyages. Medical doctors could also use the secrets behind bear hibernation to better assist bedridden patients.

The Second-Longest Glacier:

What's Nature's Version of Pancake Batter on a Griddle?

It's a glacier on an ice cap. Not surprisingly, the longest glaciers are found in Antarctica, but why in the South Pole region and not the North Pole region? Directly beneath the North Pole is the Arctic Ocean. The entire North Pole is an ocean covered by an ice cap. Antarctica is land covered by a gigantic ice cap. Lambert-Fisher Glacier is the largest and longest on the planet. It's 320 miles long and, in some locations, over 40 miles wide. This big river of ice drains 8.4 cubic miles of ice into the sea each year.

The second-longest glacier on the planet is the Byrd Glacier, named after famed polar explorer Richard Evelyn Byrd. It's 60 miles long and 12 miles wide. The Byrd Glacier drops 4,300 feet as it courses out of the Transantarctica Mountains. It holds the record for supplying more ice to the Ross Ice Shelf than any other glacier to its ice shelf in Antarctica. It also moves a half mile per year. Sound fast? Glacial scientists seem to think so. They consider the Byrd Glacier to be such a swift mover, they've named it an ice stream.

A Floating Island

Glaciers cover 11 percent of all land surfaces and hold ¾ of the world's freshwater. An amazing 90 percent of all ice is in Antarctica. When part of an ice shelf, or glacier, breaks off, an iceberg is formed. This process is called "calving." One of the largest icebergs, B-15, was 180 miles by 9 miles (that's larger than Jamaica).

Does This Ocean Make Me Look Fat?

The largest recorded size of an elephant is 13 tons. The second-largest ocean animal is the fin whale, and it tips the scales at 80 tons. You may already know the largest animal of the ocean is the blue whale, but few know much about the ocean's second-largest resident. The fin whale can grow 88 feet long and swim so fast (close to 20 mph) that early sailors called it "the greyhound of the sea." Fin whales are known to travel rapidly over vast distances; one whale covered over 1,000 miles in only five days.

The fin whale is the most common baleen whale. A baleen whale is one that opens its mouth very wide, gulps up huge volumes of water, and forces water out using its tongue. Fish and other organisms in the water get trapped in the baleen, which acts like giant combs. The fin whale has between 50 and 100 expansion pleats on its underside that run from its mouth to its navel. And yes, they are mammals, so they have an umbilical cord attached before being born. Therefore, whales must also have the largest bellybuttons on the planet—above or below the water.

Amazing Whale Facts

- The blue whale has a heart the size of a small car, but its external ear opening is the size of a pencil eraser.
- Male and female killer whale offspring stay with their mother for their lifetime. It's the only mammal other than the hardcore Trekkie that does so.
- There are two known hybrid whales: a blue/fin whale and a humpback/blue whale.

The Second-Largest Insect:

The God of Ugly Things

Who wants to learn about the dung-collecting, dung-eating, largest insect on the planet, the Goliath beetle? Enough said. The second-largest insect, the giant weta, measures more than 3 inches long (only slightly shorter than the Goliath beetle) and enjoys a feces-free diet. The giant weta is also thought to be one of the heaviest insects on Earth. Some females carrying eggs have been found weighing 2.5 ounces. The giant weta is found only on the island of New Zealand, where wetas are considered symbols of habitat conservation. To most people, they look and act like a giant grasshopper. However, they are so heavy they cannot jump. The weta is a strict vegetarian and only ventures out at night for food. It's also a talented musician, "singing" by rubbing its abdomen with its legs. But when it's time to put down the harp and pick up the hatchet, it protects itself by quickly raising its spiny, hind legs. Oh, and the "god of ugly things"? It's the English translation of *weta punga*, what New Zealand's native Maori call the giant weta.

What about a Weta-Rex?

Weta Digital is the name of the five-time Academy Award winning visual effects facility behind such films as *The Lord of the Rings* Trilogy and *Avatar*. This leader in special effects was founded by a group of New Zealand filmmakers, including Lord of the Hobbits Peter Jackson. When watching Jackson's *King Kong*, look for the weta-rexes—the weta-looking creatures crawling around Skull Island. Their appearance was based upon that of the world's second-largest insect.

Salamander and Salamini-mander

The Japanese Giant Salamander, with a length of more than 5 feet, is the second-largest amphibian in the world. The largest, the Chinese Giant Salamander, can edge him out by about one foot.

The Japanese Giant Salamander is found on the northern part of Kyushu Island and western Honshu. It's able to live in these sparse, cool conditions thanks to two of its features: an incredibly slow metabolism that allows it to go weeks without eating and its lack of gills, meaning it must consume oxygen through its skin. This requires water with high oxygen content, something the cool currents of rural Japanese streams provide.

The Japanese Giant Salamander may appear to be as gentle as a giant, but when males compete for mates, things can get crazy. Ferocious males will fight to the death in some cases. Between 400 and 500 eggs are laid by the female each year and are protected vigorously by the male. These enormous salamanders feed on aquatic life species, insects, fish, and other amphibians. The giant salamanders have very poor vision but use smell, touch, and vibration to locate prey.

An American Giant?

Yes and no. A very large salamander called the hellbender lives in the eastern United States and the Missouri and Arkansas Ozarks. Technically no giant, its 2½ feet dwarfs the standard salamander length of 4 to 8 inches. Like their giant Asian salamander cousins, hellbenders prefer cold, fast-moving mountain streams. Hellbenders are not as bad as their name implies, but they will bite if agitated. Since they're picky about their water, they're a good indicator species of water quality.

A Croc o' Something

That's a lot of croc. The Nile crocodile comes in second place as the world's largest reptile at 16 feet and 2,200 pounds. The largest reptile, at 23 feet long and 2,900 pounds, is the saltwater crocodile. But the Nile crocodile has a couple of advantages over the saltwater croc. It has superior brainpower and a more highly developed heart.

Nile crocodiles are great parents compared to other reptiles. Both males and females will rush to the aid of their young's distress signals. Once mated, the female croc finds a suitable location for her fifty or so eggs and covers them with sand. While the eggs are incubating, she'll go without food for three months so she can safeguard her subterranean nest. After the eggs hatch, she'll carry them to the river and guard them for six more months. These doting mothers have even been observed watching their offspring from the previous year.

The Croaking of a Croc-less River
The site of a Nile crocodile pulling a zebra into the water and drowning it doesn't shed a favorable light on the croc's image. But what if the crocs packed up and left? First, barbell catfish populations would explode without anything to eat them. Then, the catfish would eat all of the other fish, many of which birds rely on for food. Once the birds' food is gone, they'll leave and take their shit with them. The river depends on nutrients found in these birds' droppings to fuel plant growth. So crocs might make the Nile bloody, but without them, it'd be bloody gone.

The Second-Biggest Rock Star on the Planet

People give Mount Everest more credit than it deserves. When it comes right down to it, there isn't that much separating Everest from K2, the world's second-tallest mountain. Sure, K2 is only 28,251 feet tall next to Everest's 29,029 feet, but if you fall, the outcome will most likely be the same.

Going up, however, has proven to be a completely different story. Only 299 people have reached the summit of K2 compared to the 2,600 who have climbed Everest. In terms of degree of difficulty, Everest also shrinks significantly in K2's jagged shadow. Seventy people have died trying to climb K2, giving it a fatality rate of 27 percent. In other words, if you are attempting to climb it in a group of four climbers, one of you probably won't be making it back alive. Everest, on the other hand, has a fatality rate of just 9 percent, giving adventurers a much safer option.

The first successful trip to the top of Everest was in 1953. K2 was finally summited just over a year later. However, after that first successful summit, it took twenty-three years before a second adventurer could reach K2's heights. Not too shabby for a second-rate mountain.

Wait a Second!

If you don't believe us when we tell you how amazing K2 is, consider the words of Italian climber Fosco Maraini, who called the mountain: "...just the bare bones of a name...It makes no attempt to sound human. It is atoms and stars. It has the nakedness of the world before the first man—or of the cindered planet after the last."

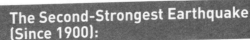

A Not-So-Good Earthquake

Earthquake vibrations can cause water-saturated soil to momentarily lose strength and act like a liquid. This process is called liquefaction. When this happens to the soil beneath buildings, they collapse. During the second-strongest earthquake ever recorded on a seismograph since 1900 (the Great Alaskan Earthquake on March 27, 1964), liquefaction caused most of the damage.

Also known as the Good Friday Earthquake, due to its timing, this Kraken of a quake shook with a magnitude of 9.2 and killed fifteen, while the subsequent tsunami took another 128 lives. Property damage was estimated to be in the neighborhood of 311 million dollars. Fortunately, since the quake struck on Good Friday when most schools and businesses were closed, few people were killed. The quake was strong enough to lift or drop a total area of around 200,800 square miles, with some places lifted as high as 38 feet and other places dropped as low as 7½ feet. The quake also produced a landside in Anchorage that displaced 130 acres.

The Strongest Earthquake Since 1900

On May 22, 1960, the Great Chilean earthquake struck with the force of 9.5 on the magnitude scale. It created a tsunami wave 82 feet high that hit the nearby Chilean coast, carrying parts of homes as far away as 2 miles inland. The monster tsunami struck Hilo, Hawaii, with a 35-foot wave and even traveled 6,000 miles to batter Japan and the Philippines with 35-foot waves. An estimated 2,000 to 6,000 people lost their lives in the earthquake and resulting tsunamis.

Fluid Seconds

Waihilau Valley is one of the few untouched and unchanged places on the northeastern coast of the big island of Hawaii. There are several spectacular waterfalls in this valley, but one of them was grand enough to name the entire valley after. Waihilau Falls, plunging 2,600 feet, is the highest waterfall in the United States and the second-highest in the world. But in the ultra competitive race for the title of the tallest waterfall, these rankings do not come without dispute.

Waihilau Falls trails behind statemates, Olo'upena Falls and Pu'uka'oku Falls, in both apostrophes and height. Then how does Waihilau Falls fall ahead in the rankings? Consistency. Unlike the other two falls, Waihilau Falls flows for most of the year, whereas the others operate only during the rainy season.

Mystified

Angel Falls in Venezuela is the highest waterfall in the world. It has a total height of 3,212 feet, but a clear drop of 2,648 feet. However, unlike the water of Waihilau Falls, the water from Angel Falls never hits the ground. Instead, the strong winds and tremendous drop obliterates the falling water into a fine mist before it can reach the end of its dive.

Rock On

Australia is home to the two largest monoliths (a single, unattached rock) in the world. For the longest time, Uluru, or Ayers Rock, was believed to be the largest. But that title now goes to Mount Augustus, also located in the Australian outback. Not only is Mount Augustus bigger than Ayers Rock—it downright crushes it by more than twice its size. But that doesn't necessarily make it a better rock. Who knows why we think of Ayers more often than Augustus when it comes to mammoth monoliths, but maybe the secret has to do with the tourists. While Mount Augustus remains a bit off the beaten path for many, tourists have been rockin' Ayers rock for more than fifty years. In fact, by the time Ayers had received UNESCO's World Heritage status in 2000, the number of annual Ayers tourists had hit 400,000. What's the point of being first if nobody sees you?

Rock 'N No Roll
Uluru, a sandstone rock, makes a striking appearance in the desert plain it calls home. Rising up 1,142 feet, stretching 2¼ miles long, spanning 1⅕ miles wide, and commanding a circumference of 5.8 miles, Uluru is one stone that will likely never be overturned. This rock also clearly has roots to the underground—only about one-seventh of it is above the surface. And just because it's too big to move doesn't mean it can't change. Over the course of a day and the seasons of a year, this rock changes colors from red to silver-gray to black stripes.

More Than Just the Amazon

The Congo rainforest is the second largest in the world and its area represents 18 percent of what remains of the world's rainforest. The water from all of the rain this amazing forest receives runs off into the world's second-largest (by volume) river, the Congo. And, with over 10,000 animal species and 600 plant species, the Congo rainforest is home to most of Africa's biodiversity. In fact, about 70 percent of all Africa's plant cover is found in the Congo Basin.

Unfortunately, the Congo rainforest is being threatened on many fronts. No region in the world has seen a higher rate of deforestation than the Congo rainforest. Civil wars, displacement of forest dwellers, and the increased "bushmeat" trade have had a very negative impact on the people and the rainforest of the Congo. Bushmeat is the meat from wild animals—usually endangered primates like the gorillas, chimps, and bonobos.

Unicorn Savior

A twelve-year-old American boy is on a mission to save the okapi, known as the African unicorn. Spencer Tait first saw the okapi at the Milwaukee Public Museum and fell in love with it. He describes the okapi as a mix between a horse and a zebra, even though it is actually related to the giraffe. Spencer, with the help of his dad, has set up a website, *www.savetheokapi.com*, to raise awareness and money for okapi preservation and research.

159 The Place with the Second Most Lightning Strikes:

It's Happened More Than Twice

The place with the second most lightning strikes is called *Relámpago del catatumbo* or, Catatumbo Lightning. Where the Catatumbo River empties into Lake Maracaibo in Venezuela, silent lightning can be observed for as long as ten hours at night. These cloud-to-cloud charges can be seen for as many as 140 to 160 nights out of a year and have been viewed from as far as 250 miles away. Catatumbo Lightning is so frequent and so bright that savvy sailors have been utilizing it as a "natural lighthouse" for hundreds of years. Considering the sublime skyline of red, yellow, and orange hues these streaks of static project, perhaps it's a miracle they haven't drawn more ships to them rather than steered them clear. Scientists believe that the lightning storms here are the largest producer of ozone in the upper altitudes on the planet. Some have even gone as far as proposing that this area be a UNESCO protected zone.

Flashy Lightning Facts

- Probably the most people killed by one lightning strike happened in 1769 in Brescia, Italy. Three thousand people were killed and one-sixth of the village was demolished when lightning struck a vault of 100 tons of gunpowder at the Church of St. Nazaire.
- Central Florida, from Tampa to Orlando, is known as the home for the most lightning strikes in the United States: more than fifty strikes per square mile happen in an average year.
- The Empire State Building in New York City seems to be a lightning rod; it gets hit about twenty-three times a year.

A Cruel Twister of Fate

May 7, 1840, at 1:00 P.M., in the town of Natchez, Mississippi, a mighty tornado blew through town, twirling mustaches and taking lives—over 317 lives to be exact. Remarkably, only forty-eight of those killed were on land when the tornado struck. If not on land, then where were the other 269 victims? On their flatboats, which they rode to the bottom of the mighty Mississip'. But since this tornado touched down in pre-Civil War Mississippi, and slave deaths would not have been counted, the actual total number of deaths is probably much higher.

While the most deadly tornado of its day, the Natchez tornado quickly fell to second after the Tri-State Tornado of 1925. The Tri-State Twister nailed three different states (Missouri, Illinois, and Indiana) and stayed on the ground for a longer distance (219 miles) and time (3½ hours) than any other tornado recorded. In total, the United States gets about 1,200 tornadoes a year compared to the 300 or so in the rest of the world.

We're Not in Dhaka Anymore

America's flyover states aren't the only place with things flying around. After the United States and Canada, more tornados turn up in Bangladesh than any other country. In fact, the two most-deadly tornados in recorded history happened in Bangladesh: the Saturia-Manikganj Sadar Tornado in 1989 took an estimated 1,300 lives, while an earlier tornado in 1969 was responsible for an estimated 923. In fact, Bangladesh has become known for its killer tornados—nineteen of its past tornados have killed a total of 100 or more people.

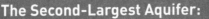

What Under Earth Is an Aquifer?

We're all walking on water—well, over it, at least. It might be hard to believe, but there's a lot of water beneath the ground we walk on. There is 100 times more water underground than in all of the lakes and rivers in the world. Gigantic areas of underground water sources are called aquifers.

The second-largest aquifer is the 463,000-square-mile Guaraní Aquifer, which lies beneath Brazil, Argentina, Paraguay, and Uruguay. It gets its name from the Guaraní tribe that lives in the area. Even though the Guaraní Aquifer is the second largest in area, it does claim to have the most volume in one place—nearly 9,000 cubic miles. Scientists believe that the volume of freshwater in the Guaraní Aquifer could supply the world's water needs for 200 years. If the anticipated shortage of freshwater happens in the near future, South America could be supplying freshwater in tanker ships to the world.

The largest is the Great Artesian Basin in Australia that covers over 656,000 square miles. Queensland and South Australia depend on this aquifer for their freshwater supply.

> **That's Depressing**
> Where's most of the United States' freshwater? A staggering 95 percent of it is underground, and most of that is found in its largest aquifer, the Ogallala, located under South Dakota, Nebraska, Kansas, Oklahoma, and Texas. The Ogallala provides water for one-fifth of all irrigated land in the United States. Ironically, most of the land affected by the 1930s Dust Bowl had billions of gallons of water under it in the Ogallala aquifer.

The Loudest Noise Ever Heard by Humans

In 1888, the Krakatau Island Volcano erupted into second place on the all-time deadliest volcano list with what is believed to have been the loudest sound ever heard by humans. The amount of force involved with Krakatau's eruption was equal to thirteen atomic bombs, and it was heard over 2,000 miles away in Perth, Australia. What goes around comes around; in spite of destroying nearly two-thirds of its island, Krakatau's eruption also created a new island: Anak Krakatau (Indonesian for, "child of Krakatau"). While it's impossible to say just how many lives Krakatau took—skeletons floating on pieces of volcanic pumice were spotted floating off the coast of East Africa close to a year after the eruption—the estimated death toll came in at 36,000.

In comparison, the deadliest volcanic eruption was Mount Tambora in Indonesia on April 10 through 15, 1816. It killed an estimated 92,000 people and threw so much ash into the air that locals would remember 1816 as "the year without a summer."

Volcanic Winter

The world's most-deadly volcanoes will probably never be known because of the lack of accurate documentation. It's believed that the Grecian volcano, Santorini, could have completely destroyed whole civilizations. Scientists have gone as far as to hypothesize that the eruption of the super-volcano Toba about 75,000 years ago could have totally decimated most of the human population by creating volcanic winters that would have lasted six to ten years. Most farm crops and animals would not have been able to survive such long, harsh winters.

Not All Rainforests Are Tropical?

Covering only a small part of the Earth, temperate rainforests exist in the temperate zones of the world where the annual rainfall is between 6 and 10 feet. No other terrestrial ecosystem has more biomass than the temperate, coniferous rainforests. They're the habitats for the Sitka Spruce, Coast Douglas Fir, and gigantic Coast Redwood. The Pacific Temperate Rainforest is the world's largest. It's located along the coast from northern California to Kodiak Island in Alaska.

Coincidentally, the continent with the largest tropical rainforest also has the second-largest temperate rainforest: South America. The Valdivian and Magellanic Temperate rainforest is located on the Pacific coast of southern Chile and on the southernmost tip of the Andes Mountains in Chile and Argentina. The largest tree in South America is not found in the Amazon rainforest but in this temperate rainforest. The Alerce is an evergreen that grows there and can reach a height of 374 feet while having a diameter of 16 feet. The world's smallest deer, the Southern Pudu; South America's smallest cat, the Kodkod; and the largest South American woodpecker, the Magellanic woodpecker, are all indigenous to the Valdivian rainforest.

Valdivian and Magellanic Rainforest

- An Alerce tree was discovered in 1993 to have tree rings that date back 3,622 years. This tree has been documented as the second-oldest tree in the world.
- The national tree of Chile, the Monkey Puzzle tree, grows in its temperate rainforest. This tree got its name from a comment made in the 1800s by an Englishman who said that it would puzzle a monkey to climb such a tree.

164 The Second-Largest Boreal Forest:

Is the Place Bor Real?

Much cooler and far less popular than rainforests, boreal forests have the Earth covered. In fact, the Canadian boreal forest is larger than the Brazilian Amazon Rainforest. Located just south of the Arctic Circle, the boreal, or *taiga* as it is commonly called, is just as important in absorbing carbon dioxide and releasing oxygen as rainforests.

Most people are not familiar with the boreal because it doesn't have the variety of flora and fauna of the rainforest. The Siberian taiga is the largest in the world, covering some 2.7 million acres. It ranges 3,542 miles from Siberia through Finland, Sweden, and Norway. The taiga covers about 600 miles from North to South. The second-largest boreal forest is the North American one; however, it's the longest at 3,853 miles. The North American boreal forest covers a semicircle from Newfoundland to Alaska on the western side. Its boundary is the tundra to the North and the Great Lakes on the South. Canada's boreal forest covers about 60 percent of its territory, but is occupied by only 14 percent of its population.

Forest Fires Are Good for the Forest
It seems counterintuitive that a fire can help a forest. First, lightning strikes are natural events that sometimes cause forest fires. These fires destroy old and diseased trees along with the pests that are harming the vegetation. Some trees, like the jack pine, depend on the heat from forest fires to open their serotinous pinecones so they can release their seeds.

The Second-Wettest Place on Earth:

Soaked Second

C oming in a close and bountiful second place for the wettest spot on Earth is Mount Waialeale. Located on the Hawaiian Island of Kauai, this sodden spot receives a yearly average of 460 inches of rainfall. Waialeale means "overflowing water" in Hawaiian, which is an understatement considering the amount of rain it receives. Mount Waialeale is no small mountain. Its altitude of more than 5,000 feet is one reason that it gets so much rain. Rain clouds don't go over Mount Waialeale, thus causing rain to fall as the clouds go around the mountain's sides. It rains almost every day on Waialeale, with only about fifty clear days a year.

Cherrapunji, India, averages above 467 inches of rain a year. But in this contest, to the victor goes no spoils. Even with all of that water, Cherrapunji still lacks a good system of irrigation, and Cherrapunjians must travel miles to get fresh water for drinking and bathing during the dry season. But when the rains get out of control, people in Cherrapunji construct "living bridges" by bending trees, roots and all, in order to cross streams. Some of their living bridges are more than 500 hundred years old.

Mountainous Measurements

A special "tipping bucket" is used to measure the rainfall on Mount Waialeale since the rain gauges are only accessible by helicopter. Rain falls in the top of the bucket and when it reaches 1/100 of an inch, the bucket tips, filling the other side of the bucket. Each tip is recorded electronically. The number of tips is then used to calculate the total rainfall.

The Second-Highest Tides:
Able to Leap over a Five-Story Building in a Single Tide

While not a popular beach destination, the second-highest tide is created in Anchorage, Alaska. The tide varies 40 feet between high and low tide, but what is most incredible is how this tide produces *bore tides*. Bore tides would rarely be described as "boring." Formed after a very low tide, when the seawater rushes in shallow and tapered coves during the beginning of the high-tide phase, these tides can create waves of 6 to 10 feet high, traveling 15 miles per hour. They generate so much power that they make noises similar to that of a locomotive.

On the opposite side of the North American continent in the Bay of Fundy's Minas Basin in Nova Scotia, Canada, the recorded range between high and low tide is 54.6 feet. During one phase of this tide, the tidal flow was equal to the flow of all rivers and streams on the planet. The Nova Scotia countryside actually tips when the 14 billion gallons of water come in with the tide.

Putting the "Tide" Back into Tidal Waves
Bore waves are considered true tidal waves since they are caused by the tides, unlike tsunamis, which are cause by seismic events. The largest bore tide is thought to be on the Tsientang River in China. It has been known to rise 30 feet and can travel at 20 mph. Some brave fools surf on these bore waves in what thrill-seekers and idiots alike refer to as river surfing.

Not a New Line of Swimwear...

The Tonga Trench, located just north of the North Island of New Zealand, is home to the second-deepest ocean trench. This trench's Horizon Deep goes down to 35,702 feet below sea level. The Tonga Trench happens to reside in a subduction zone: an area where two or more tectonic plates are being sunk into the mantle where rock melts back into lava-hot magma. Not only is this trench hot, but it's also a quick mover; at 10 inches a year, the Tonga Trench moves faster than any other trench plate on the planet. All that getting around doesn't come without its downside: Tonga is the number one deep earthquake creator in the world. The Tonga Trench also provides a solution for the next time you are looking for a place to dispose of any radioactive material you might have lying around. After the Apollo 13 debacle left NASA with the lunar module's battery intact, they sunk it to the depths of the Tonga Trench. Maybe, that's why so many deep-sea fish glow.

Not So Well Rounded

It would make sense that the deepest point in the ocean—Challenger Deep of the Mariana Trench—would also be the closest to the center of the Earth. But this isn't the case. Flattening off at the poles and bulging at the equator like a football, Earth is far from a perfect sphere. Parts of the Arctic Ocean seafloor are about 43,000 feet closer to the center of the Earth than Challenger Deep.

The farthest surface point away from the Earth's center? Mount Chimborazo in Ecuador.

The Second-Fastest Ocean Current:

A Current Debate

Religion and politics aren't the only things people can find to disagree on. A fierce debate over which ocean current is the fastest is currently raging among members of the scientific community. In one corner flows the Gulf Stream; this current runs from the eastern coast of the United States and Canada across the Atlantic to Europe. In the other corner is the lesser-known Agulhas Current. This current flows from the eastern coast of South Africa through the Indian Ocean to where it meets the Southern Ocean before turning back into the Indian Ocean. Thanks to its immense range, the Agulhas Current is considered to be in first place when it comes to the total amount of water moved.

So, if scientists can measure these currents' volumes and distances, why the debate over their speed? Because the speeds of currents change with the seasons. The currents' identical speeds in specific locations during certain times have caused scientists to debate which current is the quickest.

Current Express Mail

Benjamin Franklin was one of the first people to make a detailed map of the Gulf Stream. While not a sailor, Franklin was a scientist and postmaster of the American colonies. After experimenting with variations in water temperatures during a trip to Europe, Franklin began to suspect that there was a current running through the ocean. This discovery provided him with an answer for why it took longer to receive mail from Europe than to send it. This current, much like a river, only flowed in one direction. Ships sped up when traveling with the current, but slowed down when traveling against it.

90 Degrees East, Two Miles Down

What exactly is a subglacial lake? Quite simply, it is a lake under ice. Antarctica has more than 145 subglacial lakes. The second-largest subglacial lake is named 90 Degrees East. Why the name that sounds more like a Manhattan nightclub than an under-ice lake? 90 Degrees East refers to the lake's longitudinal location. At 772 square miles in total size, 90 Degrees East is a distant number two in comparison to Lake Vostok's gargantuan 5,400 square miles. Not only is this lake not 90°F, it's not even close; its water checks in at a frigid 27°F. How can water with a temperature below freezing keep from turning into ice? It is able to maintain its balmy (compared to temperatures reaching as low as -112°F on the surface of Antarctica) climate due to a combination of tremendous pressure exerted on it from the weight of nearly two miles of ice above it and the warmth of geothermal forces from the Earth's crust just below it.

Do Not Disturb
Lake Vostok's water is supersaturated with oxygen. The water has fifty times more dissolved oxygen than surface lakes and is under incredible pressure. Scientists believe that oxygen and other gases are trapped inside the lattice of certain molecules. If scientists would drill into the lake, the water would spurt out as if they had dropped a roll of Mentos into a bottle of Diet Coke.

Asia Is Not the Biggest in Everything

W hat's the discrepancy in size between the world's largest land animal and the next largest? The second largest could fit inside of the largest with room to spare. What are these two animals? Elephants—both of them. How big are elephants? So big that they take both first and second place on the list of the world's largest land animals. The second place Asian elephant is still a big deal at 11,000 pounds, 9½ feet. But it is downright tiny compared to its larger cousin, the African elephant, which lumbers in at 27,000 pounds, 27½ feet. Just as remarkable as their size, both species of elephants have as many as 100,000 muscles in their trunks alone!

If you're curious as to what the second-largest non-elephant land animal is, it is the white rhinoceros. It measures in at 7,920 pounds and 12½ feet long.

Extreme Recyclers

Not only are Asian elephants the second-largest land animals, they also don't mind eating food the second time around. That's right, due to a unique, evolutionary gift, Asian elephants are among a handful of animals known as "dung eaters" who are able to consume and derive nutrients from feces. Other members of this selective society include rabbits, koalas, and of course, the dung beetle.

The Second-Largest Invertebrate:

What's Bigger, a Giant or a Colossus?

When it comes to squids, scientists still aren't sure. So far, these stealthy sea creatures have been too elusive for scientists to definitively rank squid size. Generally, though, the colossal squid is thought to be the largest squid in the world with an estimated length of 45 feet.

But the giant squid is putting up a strong fight. These deep-sea monsters are 35 feet long with eight arms—each lined with two rows of suckers—and two, longer tentacles. The largest giant squid ever found, though, was 59 feet long and weighed almost 2,000 pounds, which makes it longer than the colossal squid. The suckers on the giant squid's arms have small teeth on the inside of them, giving them the appearance of circular saw blades. The colossal squid has an even more amazing sucker feature: hooks that swivel inside their suckers. Both squids also come equipped with eyes as large as soccer balls and built-in "headlights." They have structures in their eyes called photophores that produce bioluminescent light. Using the light produced by these "headlights," squids can see through the dark ocean depths.

When Squids Attack

The colossal squid keeps its arms and tentacles above its head most of its life. Scientists call this the "cockatoo" position. This position allows the squid to use its "headlights" in spotting potential prey. Once it has spotted its prey, the squid first uses its rotating, hooked tentacles to grab hold of its victim. After pulling it into its arms, the arms bring it to the mouth before letting its beak-like jaws do the rest.

Butterflies as Big as Birds

T he second-largest butterfly comes in first place for impressive names: the Goliath birdwing. While slightly smaller than the first-place Queen Alexandra's birdwing, the Goliath, with a wingspan of 11 inches, is still no gnat. The Goliath birdwing is found in Papua New Guinea, where the locals raise the butterflies for sale. With a permit, it's legal for locals to farm them. Sure, professional butterfly wrangler might not be the most masculine occupation, but someone has to do it. Besides, it can be pretty profitable. The government has even regulated how many Goliath birdwings leave the country. The butterflies' values are the reason why: mounted in a picture frame, they can cost as much as $225 each. The Queen Alexandra's birdwing specimen can cost as much as $10,000.

The Queen Alexandra's birdwing, the world's biggest butterfly, has a 1-foot wingspan. How does such a large butterfly avoid being eaten by predators? Like many other swallowtail butterflies, the birdwing caterpillars eat plants that contain poison but do not kill it. The poison stays in the caterpillar as it grows into an adult butterfly, making it lethal to any would-be predators.

A Leading Leper

All butterflies and moths belong to the Lepidoptera order of insects. People who collect butterflies call themselves "lepers." One of the most famous lepers is Justin "Tiny" Nuyda of the Philippines. One method Tiny uses is to spike rotten pineapples with rum. After butterflies suck up the laced juice, they become disoriented and much easier to catch with bare hands. Tiny's butterflies have even been featured on some of the Philippine's postal stamps.

The Second-Largest Cold Desert:

Pretty Cool

The second-largest cold desert is the Patagonian Desert, located primarily in a country you don't necessarily equate with being cold: Argentina. It holds the record as the largest desert of any kind in North or South America with an area of 260,000 square miles. The Patagonian Desert's seasons are seven months of winter and five months of summer, and the temperature range is from a summer high of 54 degrees Fahrenheit to a low of 37 degrees Fahrenheit in the winter.

Gobi, the largest cold desert, lies mainly in southern Mongolia. It's the fifth-largest of all deserts with an area of 500,000 square miles. The Gobi is known for its temperature extremes; the spread is 104 degrees Fahrenheit in the summer and –40 degrees Fahrenheit in the dead of winter. The Great Gobi National Park is home to the wild two-humped Bactrian camels and the only desert-dwelling bears, the Gobi bears.

Along the Patagonian Desert coast, a traveler might come across an animal rather unexpected in a desert: a penguin. The Magellanic penguin, to be precise. Other animals that inhabit the Patagonian are the guanaco (a cousin of the llama); the lesser rhea, a large flightless bird (a cousin of the emu and ostrich); the tuco-tuco (a rodent); and the pygmy armadillo, the smallest armadillo.

Desert Penguins

Some penguins never even visit Antarctica. Magellanic penguins are temperate climate penguins and live off the coast of Chile, Argentina, and some nearby islands. The Magellanic penguin is called the *jackass penguin*, not because it's crazy enough to reside in the desert, but because its call sounds like the braying of a donkey.

A Coral Corral

Atolls are some of the most amazing landmasses in the oceans. They're made of coral reef that surrounds a lagoon. The second-largest atoll is the Aldabra Atoll located in the Indian Ocean, about 700 miles from the main island of the Seychelles, Mahe, and 265 miles northwest of Madagascar.

Only the second-biggest atoll, it enjoys the distinction of being on the UNESCO list of World Heritage Sites. Also, due to its elevation of just over 26 feet, the Aldabra Atoll holds the world record for the largest raised coral reef. The atoll is uninhabited by humans, which probably explains why the animal life thrives and remains so well protected. The atoll has more giant tortoises than the more famous Galapagos Islands. In fact, the Aldabra Atoll is home to about 100,000 giant tortoises—another world record. The world's largest land crab, the coconut crab, is also indigenous to the atoll. The atoll's bird life even includes the Indian Ocean's last surviving flightless bird, the Aldabra rail. The largest atoll is the Kiritimati Atoll, which also goes by the cheery misnomer of Christmas Island.

One Clean Atoll

Aldabra Atoll is home to ten scientists who monitor changes in the corals and other animal life. They're helping keep the island in its pristine and natural state. They hope the atoll can serve as a bellwether for the rest of the world's coral reef communities. Due to its remoteness and harsh terrestrial environment, the atoll has been kept free from much of human exploration and exploitation.

The Second-Largest Coral Reef:

Caribbean Queen

One of the most incredible biomes in the world is the coral reef, and anyone with a snorkel knows that the largest reef in the world is the Great Barrier Reef off the northeast coast of Australia. Little known to most Americans, however, is the "Jewel of the Caribbean": a huge, pristine, and diverse coral reef to our south that is also the second-largest coral reef on the planet. Its official name is the Mesoamercian Barrier Reef, and it stretches 700 miles from the coast of Mexico, down along the coasts of Belize, Guatemala, and Honduras. It's the largest reef in the western hemisphere and is extremely important in protecting the coastline from storms and erosion. Within the Mesoamerican Barrier Reef are several parks and reserves, and it needs several reserves to help protect the more than 500 species of fish, 350 species of mollusks, and 65 species of corals that live there. The reef also might prove to be the final home for one of Earth's most interesting creatures, the manatee. With estimated populations at between 1,000 and 1,500 of the sea cows, the Mesoamerican Barrier Reef is one of the manatees' most populous spots.

The Ins and Outs of Coral Reefs

- Reefs are home to 25 percent of all ocean fish species but only cover 1 percent of the Earth's surface.
- Half a billion people depend directly on coral reefs for their food and livelihoods.
- Some kinds of coral skeletons have been used in human bone grafts.

The Great Krait Snake

Kraits are part of the cobra family. This family is characterized by two features: short fangs and lethal venom. Out of the twelve species of snakes in this family, it's the common krait that strikes second on the list of deadliest snakes in the world. Milligram per milligram, its venom is among the most toxic of all snakes. It takes just 0.5 milligrams of this krait's killing juice to deliver a lethal blow to a human. Injecting 84 milligrams of venom per bite, this snake is capable of wiping out forty-two people in a single strike.

Scientists have observed that these snakes barely function during daylight hours. But once evening sets, these kraits transform from zombies into full-blown vampires. Reportedly, 75 percent of people bitten by a common krait don't get a second chance. One of the main reasons for its lethal efficiency is believed to be its relatively painless bite. Victims often either feel no pain or assume the bite to have come from a non-venomous snake. This false sense of security can stall victims from seeking anti-venom, thereby significantly lessening the effectiveness of the anti-venom.

Snakes on Our Side

Able to kill 120 humans with a single bite, the coastal taipan is the planet's deadliest snake. But, in the long run, their venom might prove to do humans more good than harm. Australian scientists have discovered that the coastal taipan's venom produces a blood-clotting agent called Factor X. There's a good chance that Factor X is just scratching the surface of the myriad potential sources of pharmaceutical components snake venom might provide.

The Second-Most-Deadly Spider:

Dangerous Bananas

B anana pickers have to be careful when they cut the banana cluster from the plant because the deadliest spider, the Banana Spider, just might be hiding in the bunch. Fortunately, an anti-venom has been developed for the Banana spider's bite.

The second-most-deadly spider is the Sydney funnel-web spider, found in eastern Australia. It only grows to two inches in size, but who needs size when you've got such fast acting and highly toxic venom? Males are known to wander extensively during their seasonal hunt for females; this behavior often brings them in contact with Sydney's residents in their homes, sheds, and gardens. When confronted, most spiders will run away, but not the Sydney funnel-web. Instead, it rears up on its back legs and shows its fangs. Apparently, all have not heeded its warning. There have been thirteen recorded deaths from the bite of the male Sydney funnel-web in the last 100 years. Anti-venom for the spider's bite became available in 1981 and since then, there have not been any recorded fatalities. The Sydney funnel-web spiders have been found in a 75-mile radius around Sydney.

Milk This

The Australia Reptile Center in Sydney has a funnel-web spider venom-milking station where people can bring in funnel-web spiders to have their venom extracted to make anti-venom. So far, about forty spiders have been turned in by the public. The anti-venom is important because the spider bite can kill in less than two hours.

Look Out Below!

Who'd want to live near Peru's highest peak, the 22,205-foot extinct volcano, Nevados Huascaran? It's been the site of the two worst avalanches in the world. An earthquake with a magnitude of 7.7 triggered the most catastrophic avalanche in history on May 31, 1970. It completely destroyed the city of Yungay, killing nearly 18,000 people. The second-worst avalanche occurred on the same mountain on January 10, 1962, when a chunk of ice from Glacier 511 the size of a skyscraper slid down the mountain's slope for 12 miles with 353,000,000 cubic feet of snow in tow. It destroyed eight small towns and the city of Ranrahirca, claiming at least 4,000 lives. The devastation was compounded by the fact that the avalanche's house-sized blocks of ice knocked loose millions of tons of rocks and mud as it grew larger and larger with each passing moment. The avalanche only lasted eight minutes and appeared as a gigantic rug, 1½ miles wide and with shag 40 feet deep, unrolling across the valley. Ranrahirca was rebuilt, but it was destroyed for a second time by another avalanche in 1970.

Worst. Train Ride. Ever!

The worst avalanche in the United States happened in the Cascade Mountains in Wellington, Washington, in 1910 when two trains became snowbound at Stevens Pass. Snow was falling at a rate of one foot an hour when a lightning storm hampered all rescue efforts. In the middle of the night, an avalanche carrying large trees and boulders slammed into the trains, forcing them down a 150-foot gorge. A total of ninety-six people on board were killed.

The Second-Longest Snake:

Slithering into Second

The longest snake in the world ever found was the Asiatic (Burmese) reticulated python. It was 33 feet long. The second-longest snake every captured was the green anaconda at 28 feet long. Even though the python is longer than the anaconda, anacondas are more massive and have the girth of a grown man—the largest being 44 inches around! Anacondas are found in the swamps and marshes of the Amazon and Orinoco river basins of Northern and Eastern South America. These super-sized snakes belong to the boa constrictor family. Constrictors are not venomous, so they've got to get even closer to their victims—by coiling around them and squeezing them—before they devour them. Once the anaconda gets its prey in its clutches, it keeps its snake-grip strong until the final countdown for its victim has begun. As the stale air exits its lungs, the victim becomes more and more bite-sized. At last, the prey suffocates or dies of internal bleeding, and dinner is served. An anaconda swallows its prey whole by unhinging its bottom jaws.

My Anaconda Don't Want None Unless You Got Seconds, Hun
The mating process for these snakes looks more like a wrestling pay-per view than late-night cable. The miracle of life all starts when anywhere from two to a dozen male anacondas coil around a female, forming what scientists refer to as a "breeding ball." The snakes then slither around as they compete for the right to mate with the female. How long does this slow-motion wrestling match last? Anywhere from two to four weeks!

Buzzzzzzzzzzzzzzoom

The second-fastest insect is the hawk moth, which tops out at 33.7 miles per hour. The hawk moths (aka sphinx moths) are the speedsters in the moth family. Some are also considered the "hummingbirds" of moths because of their incredible hovering ability. These moths have an aerodynamic, bullet-shaped body with slender forewings and shorter back wings. This sleek design helps them travel as fast and far as they do.

Hawk moths are known as important pollinators for orchids, lavender, and phlox. Typically, they pollinate flowers that open at night and are white or pale in color. Like all moths, they feed on the nectar from flowers by using their proboscis—a long, hollow feeding tube that serves as a mouth. The proboscis then coils back into their head when they're not feeding. Most flowers in North America have 2-inch nectar tubes, but luckily hawk moths have a 2⅓ inch proboscis. The larvae of most North American hawk moths have a "horn" on their rear end, leading to their sometimes being referred to as *hornworms*. With cruising speeds hitting 35 miles per hour, dragonflies are the fastest flying insects—but they're not nearly as scary.

Don't Bee Afraid, Clarisse

One of the more famous hawk moths is the death's head, which looks like it has a skull on its back. This moth was featured in the movie *The Silence of the Lambs*. One species of the death's head hawk moth has been seen in England around beehives feeding on honey. Incredibility, the bees do not harm the moth. It's believed that the moth transmits a sound that mimics the sound of the queen bee, thereby protecting it.

PART 5

Sports: Second Place *Is* More Than First Loser

When it comes to sports, or any competition for that matter, it's easy to disregard second-place finishers. We don't play for second place, we play for keeps. You've heard all of the clichés before. But is there more? Should we be so quick to banish second place finishers because they lost in their final game? Or, for individual athletes, should we ignore one's efforts—not to mention accomplishments—just because there was a single person (arguably) better? You be the judge. But we think it will surprise you to find out just how much was done, failing to be number one. Seconds, you're winners in our book!

The Second Marathon:

When 26.2 Was Just a Warm Up

A round 490 B.C., during the Greco-Persian Wars, the Persians were going to attack the Grecian city-state of Athens. The Athenian military decided to send a professional runner, Phidippides, to the Grecian city-state of Sparta to ask for military help. Sparta had a strong army and was well trained in the art of war. Phidippides ran 140 miles over rock and uneven ground to Sparta in thirty-six hours, but the Spartans were unable to come to Athens's aid at the time.

This first marathon is often forgotten. It is the *second* marathon everyone thinks of first. You probably know that the best-known marathon was run by the same man, Phidippides, who ran the *first* marathon. Even though it was a much shorter distance, it was here, after his second battlefield jaunt, that the race got its name. I guess they thought Spartathon didn't have the same ring to it.

When the Athenians realized that they could not rely on Sparta for assistance, they sent out a small army (that would be outnumbered four to one) to the plains of Marathon to attack the Persians. The Athenian army was victorious, and Phidippides ran the 26 miles back to Athens to tell of the victory and the impending attack from the sea by the retreating Persians. Phidippides gave the report and then died from exhaustion.

Prepare for Glory

Have you ever heard of the Spartathlon? It's an ultramarathon race held every year since 1983 from Athens to Sparta, at a distance of 152 miles. Racers must finish in the thirty-six-hour time slot allowed or return home in shame.

Hank Aaron, Second to None

Whether the mere mention of his name causes you to shudder as if in a fit of 'roid-rage or not, baseball has a new homerun king. But rather than debating the validity or worthiness of Barry Bonds, why not celebrate the man he is turning into a second?

When looking back over his myriad accomplishments, we often overlook several facts that made "Hammerin' Hank" so great. Aaron failed in his first attempt to break into the majors. In 1949, at the age of fifteen, he tried out, unsuccessfully, for the Brooklyn Dodgers. It wasn't until his *second* attempt that he made it to the big leagues. Not only did Aaron have to overcome the physical demands of his sport, but he also had to persevere through racial hurdles placed in his path. Hank Aaron was also a last. He was the last Negro League player to play in Major League Baseball. As a part of the Mobile Black Bears, Aaron was paid ten dollars a game.

Hank wasn't just known for hammering the ball. He's on the short list of baseball's 30/30 men (someone who hits at least 30 homeruns and steals at least 30 bases). And, even though Pete Rose pushed Hank from number two in most base hits, he continues to lead all players in RBIs, extra-base hits, and total bases.

Hall of Snubs

In spite of his Herculean feats, Hank Aaron was still left off nine of the ballots for his selection to the Hall of Fame. It'll be interesting to see how that compares to Bonds's ballot when he becomes eligible in 2013.

183 Second-Generation Teams:

Who's on Second?

The New York Yankees weren't always the Yankees—and they didn't always play in New York. The Yankees of today began as the Baltimore Orioles of yesteryear, or 1901 to be exact. After spending two years in Baltimore, the Orioles moved to the Bronx. The move also brought with it a new name, the New York Highlanders. The Yankees remained the Highlanders for a decade until 1913, when they adopted their current moniker.

So, what about those Baltimore Orioles? How are there Orioles in Baltimore today if they left for New York over a century ago? Try to follow along for a second: the Milwaukee Brewers left Milwaukee in 1902 for St. Louis, where they became that city's second Major League franchise. St. Louis's original baseball team had recently taken its third name, the Cardinals. So, the Brewers took their franchise's second name, the Browns—which happened to be the first name of the Cardinals. After playing in St. Louis for fifty-two seasons, the Browns moved to Baltimore to become the Orioles—the city's second Orioles franchise. What happened to Milwaukee? In 1969, the Seattle Pilots took off and landed in Milwaukee as the Brewers for that city's second Brewers' franchise.

Yankee Stadium Strikes Back

The New York Yankees currently play in their second Yankee Stadium. The 2009 Yankees were also the second team to win a World Series during their first year in a new stadium. The first team to do that was the 2006 St. Louis Cardinals, the same Cardinals who are perched behind the Yankees at number two for all-time World Series wins with ten.

Second-Place Golfer:

Chump or Champ?

At the 2010 Chicagoland Collegiate Athletic Conference Championship, it was the second-place finisher, Grant Whybark, who briefly won the attention of the nation. With Whybark's University of St. Francis having already wrapped up the team championship, he found himself in a playoff with Olivet Nazarene's Seth Doran to determine the individual winner of the tournament. Since spots to the National Championship were awarded to both the winning team and individual winner, Whybark's spot in the championship was secured. So on the first tee, Whybark shot his ball about 40 yards out of bounds and went on to double-bogey the hole thereby allowing Doran, who parred the hole, to take the individual title and move on to the National Championship. Afterwards, Whybark claimed, "Somehow, it just wasn't in my heart to try to knock him out."

Major Major

The second-oldest major professional golf tournament is the U.S. Open. It was established in 1895, thirty-five years after the first Open Championship (or, British Open). Held in June, the U.S. Open is also the second major tournament on the PGA schedule. It's also unique among all majors in that it doesn't go to a playoff in the case of a tie. Instead, it has an entire eighteen-hole round the following day to determine the winner. If this fifth round results in a tie, it goes to a sudden-death playoff—something that has happened only three times.

Super Seconds

Super Bowl II, on January 14, 1968, in Miami Florida, was viewed by an estimated 39.12 million people, a thirty-second commercial spot cost $54,000, and the halftime entertainment was the Grambling State University Band. It also had a couple of notable seconds: the Green Bay Packers won their second title, and quarterback Bart Starr won his second Super Bowl MVP award—tying him for second (along with Terry Bradshaw and Tom Brady) for the most Super Bowl MVPs. The game was also the last game Vince Lombardi ever coached for the Packers. Not long after the game, Lombardi retired as head coach and the Packers' general manager. But after just a year, he became the first legendary Packer to come out of retirement for another team. In 1969, Lombardi coached the Washington Redskins to a 7-5-2 record, their first winning season in fourteen years.

Super Bowl II is often overshadowed by the NFC Championship game that put the Packers in the Super Bowl—the infamous "Ice Bowl" against the Dallas Cowboys at Lambeau Field in Green Bay, Wisconsin. Famous for its freezing temperatures (-13 degrees Fahrenheit with a wind chill of -48 degrees Fahrenheit) as much as its dramatic finale, the "Ice Bowl" is considered by many football aficionados as the greatest game in NFL history.

The Band Plays On
Just like the Packers, Super Bowl II wasn't Grambling State's first trip to the game. Having played the first Super Bowl, Grambling State would go on to perform at two more—enough to become the second-most-frequent performer in Super Bowl history. Only Up with People has more.

The Second-Oldest Public Golf Course in the United States:

Another Boston-New York Sports Rivalry

The William J. Devine Golf Course at Franklin Park in Dorchester, Massachusetts, is the second-oldest public course in the United States, but it leads in public golfing lore. Opened in 1896, the course has been recognized by *Golf World* magazine as being one of the best in 2007, 2008, and 2009. Many famous golfers have played on the course, including Willie Campbell, the first to win America's first professional match; Bobby Jones, who was one of the first champion golfers; and George F. Grant, the inventor of the golf tee. The course was designed by Donald J. Ross, probably the world's best golf architect and one of the most influential course designers of the time. The William J. Devine Golf Course is considered to be a part of the Emerald Necklace: a chain of a green beltway of parks and natural areas going halfway around Boston.

The oldest public golf course is found in the Bronx. The Van Cortlandt Park Golf Course opened in 1895 and is still in operation today. It is especially noted for its second hole, a 600+ yard monster.

That's a Lot of Holes.
Even though most have probably never heard of Donald J. Ross, modern golfers owe him a great deal of credit. This Scottish import spent his life's savings to get to the United States. Once here, he designed over 413 golf courses, including such gems as Pinehurst No. 2 (host to three U.S. Opens and one PGA Championship) in North Carolina, Oak Hill (three U.S. Opens and two PGA Championships) in New York, and Oakland Hills (six U.S. Opens and three PGA Championships) outside of Detroit.

The Second-Most-Popular Sport in the World:

A Popular Sport You've Never Played

Cricket is beaten by only soccer as the world's most popular sport. It's played in more than 130 countries and by an estimated 3 billion people. India is the most popular cricket-playing country and is home to several of the sport's top players. Most Indians play cricket, watch cricket, or at least talk about it in one way or another. Considering that there are 1.3 billion Indians, its population somewhat inflates the popularity of the sport. Cricket had its beginning in southern England in the 1500s, and by the 1700s it had become the national sport of England. This is how cricket went on to become America's first stick-and-ball game; between 1834 and 1914, the United States had more than 1,000 cricket clubs. Times have changed, and now America's largest and most diverse city, New York, has fewer than 1,000 players.

Cricket Versus Baseball

Cricket might be baseball's elder cousin, but they don't share much beyond a ball and a bat: cricket players run with their bats, bowlers (pitchers) sprint before bowling the ball, fielders do not have gloves, and there is no foul territory. Spitballs are permitted in cricket, and when the bowler throws the ball, the ball hits the ground first and spins before it reaches the batsman. When a batsman hits a ball over the boundary (a homerun in baseball), it's called a six.

Double-Dribble

Perhaps the most notorious number two NBA draft pick is Sam Bowie of the 1984 draft. Picked after Hakeem Olajuwon and before Michael Jordan, Bowie is now considered by many as the biggest bust in NBA draft history. If it weren't for Ryan Leaf (the number two pick in the 1998 NFL draft), Bowie might be considered the biggest draft bust of all-time.

In spite of his many firsts, if anyone were to appreciate the value of "seconds," Michael Jordan would be the man. Forget for a second his scoring titles, championships, and endorsements, and think about the Emsley A. Laney High School fighting Bucs, Jordan's first team. Michael Jordan got cut the first time he tried out for the varsity basketball team. So what did he do? Rather than hitting the links, he hit the gym and worked on his game in order to make the most out of his second tryout the following year. Needless to say, he made the team on his second time around. Then, he went on to be one of the first two-time, three-peaters in NBA history.

Tragic Seconds

Len Bias, number two overall pick in the 1986 draft, was found dead the day after draft day from a cocaine overdose. Bias's legacy sadly morphed from one of the most anticipated players in NBA history into a cautionary tale of wasted talent and the recklessness of youth.

A list of famous (and infamous) second picks since 1986 A.B. (After Bowie): Jason Kidd, Stromile Swift, Jay Williams, Darko Milicic, LaMarcus Aldridge, Kevin Durant, and Hasheem Thabeet.

The Second-Longest Major League Baseball Game:

Take Me Home from the Ball Game

Baseball players actually worked an eight-hour day (and six minutes of overtime) on May 8, 1984, when the Chicago White Sox played the Milwaukee Brewers in a twenty-five-inning game that took two days to complete. The game was stopped after seventeen innings at 12:59 A.M. and resumed before their game the next day. The Sox won 7 to 6.

The second-longest Major League baseball game was played about ten years earlier when the St. Louis Cardinals played the New York Mets after a seven-hour-and-four-minute, twenty-five-inning duel. Second in total time, the game managed to wrap up a few firsts of its own. A record 175 official at-bats was established. In all, forty-five runners were left on base—another record. The game is also the longest night game ever played in Major League Baseball. Since the National League didn't have a curfew rule like the Chicago–Milwaukee game, the contest continued on into the wee hours of the morning. Coincidentally, this game holds the record for the longest game to reach a decision without a suspension of play. The game finished at 3:13 A.M. after a couple of Met errors let in the winning run.

Let's Play Two...Days
The longest professional baseball game ever played was a Triple-A game between the Pawtucket Red Sox and the Rochester Red Wings. The game lasted thirty-three innings. The first thirty-two innings were played from Saturday afternoon until a little after 4 A.M. the next morning. It was then resumed the following Tuesday when Pawtucket needed just one inning to end it.

Stinking Ships

The one thing sports fans like to do more than celebrate their team's dynasty is to bitch about their curses. As with practically everything in sports—except the final score—how much a franchise sucks is subjective. But that didn't stop Monte Burke of Forbes.com from trying. After his investigation of teams from all four major sports, Burke ranked the Los Angeles Clippers as the second-worst sports franchise going. As if the Clippers' six winning seasons out of a total of forty wasn't enough to award them a top spot, Burke was thorough enough to conclude that there is actually a franchise *worse* than the Clippers. That's right, the Memphis Grizzlies! What also makes matters worse for the Clippers is the fact that they share their home with the NBA's second-most-successful team, the Lakers. It's not the SoCo sunshine that keeps their fans away—they just stink. Forbes values the Clippers at just $295 million. Now $295 million is a lot of money—that is, unless you play in the second-largest television market in the country. Then it just becomes 295 million reasons why you suck. Perhaps, 295 million is a better number than .362, though—that's the Clipper's franchise winning percentage.

Do Bears Shit in Gyms?
Apparently, bears from Vancouver and Memphis do. When it comes to misery, who cares about number two, just get to the worst. The same Forbes report lists the Memphis Grizzlies as the number one-worst sports franchise. With a winning percentage of .332, the Grizzlies can say they're number one at something: losing.

191 The Second Athlete to Receive the Presidential Medal of Freedom:

Here's to Two, Joe DiMaggio

The second person to receive the Presidential Medal of Freedom was New York Yankee baseball player Joe DiMaggio. Joe is best remembered by baseball fans for his record fifty-six-game hitting streak. To this day, it has yet to be broken. Joe was such a dominant player that he was an All-Star in each of his thirteen seasons. The "Yankee Clipper," as Joe was affectionately called, wore the Yankee pinstripes for his entire baseball career. His slugging percentage is among the highest in baseball history.

The first athlete to be awarded the Presidential Medal of Freedom was Olympic champion Jesse Owens. Owens was awarded the medal by President Gerald Ford in 1976—but he didn't bag Marilyn Monroe.

A Hero on Several Fronts

Off the field, DiMaggio was best known for marrying the most glamorous movie star of the time, Marilyn Monroe. She was his second wife (actress Dorothy Arnold was his first). They divorced within a year, but they remained close until her death in 1962. But DiMaggio should also be remembered for his service to his country. As remarkable as his stats are, who knows what they could have been had DiMaggio not traded the Yankees for the military when he enlisted at the peak of his prime during World War II.

Que les jeux commencent!

The second city to host the modern Olympics was Paris. Unfortunately for the games, 1900 was a busy year for Paris. Of course, the recently built Eiffel Tower was a larger attraction than the Olympic Games. But who would have guessed the Olympics lost out to Paris World's Fair in total attendance? While Olympic organizers did a fine job making sure the World's Fair and the Olympics would occur at the same time and place every four years, the Olympics themselves were not very organized. The games lasted for five months and were held at different locations throughout France. Since the Games were so under-promoted, many athletes were not even aware that they could take part in the Olympics.

American Alvin Kraenzlein was the star of the games, winning four events: 60-meter dash, 110-meter hurdles, 200-meter hurdles, and the long jump. The French captured many medals, partly because many events had only French participants. Yet, some events even had participants from different countries on the same teams. Many events at the Paris games, such as rugby, polo, cricket, croquet, golf, and tug of war, are no longer a part of today's games.

In 1896, Athens, home of the original Olympic Games, held the first Olympics of the modern era.

Pioneer Without a Prize

The Olympics in Paris did achieve a rather notable first: they were the first Olypmic Games to allow women to compete. Charlotte Cooper is considered to be the first woman to medal; she won the women's tennis competition. The only problem was, medals weren't awarded until the 1924 games.

The Second-Most-Engraved Name on the Stanley Cup:

Two Scoring Richards

L ord Stanley's Cup has the name of Jean Beliveau engraved on it seventeen times. Ten of those are as a player on the Montreal Canadiens and seven as a member of management in the Canadiens' front office.

The second-most-engraved name is Henri Richard with eleven. In 1955, Maurice "Rocket" Richard brought his kid brother, Henri, to the Canadiens' training camp. At first, people thought it was a publicity stunt, but Henri soon proved them wrong. He was even told that he was too small by Elmer Lach, his junior coach. Henri was not an overpowering player, but he was a creative, skilled, stick-handling player with great leadership skills which came from his determination and being a team player. Henri was also known as one of the most relentless forecheckers in the history of the game. Maurice was a tremendous goal-scoring machine himself (544 to Henri's 358); even though Henri did not get as much attention as his older brother, he was the more complete player. Henri played more seasons (20 to Maurice's 18), played in more games (1,256 to 978), scored more playoff points (129 to 126), scored more total points (1046 to 965), and the crowning achievement: more Stanley Cups (11 to 8).

Cup Check

- The Stanley Cup was made in Sheffield, England, in 1892, for the price of $48.67.
- It's the only trophy passed from player to player of the winning team during the summer after their win.
- It's the only trophy with the names of players, coaches, and staff engraved on it.
- There are ten misspellings on it; most notably, Boston is spelled "Bqstqn."

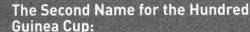

194

The Second Name for the Hundred Guinea Cup:

132 to 3ip

I n 1851, British yachtsmen challenged Americans to a yacht race for the Royal Yacht Squadron's Hundred Guinea Cup. The winning boat was the *America*, which outran fifteen British yachts around the Isle of Wight. The commodore, John Cox Stevens, brought the trophy back to the United States and donated it to the New York Yacht Club. The cup was to be a "perpetual challenge cup for friendly competition between foreign countries." The cup was then given its second name, "The America's Cup." But the trophy gets its name for the yacht, not the country. Then again, from what does the yacht get its name? Oh, well. The yacht club with the trophy becomes the defender, with all eligible yacht clubs challenging to win the America's Cup.

Immediately after the cup was announced, European yacht clubs members were confronted with a substantial problem: they had to build a yacht heavy enough to cross the Atlantic but light enough to be able to win the race. As a result, the United States kept the cup for the next 132 years in what many consider the longest winning streak in any sport. The streak was broken in 1983, when *Australia II* beat America's *Liberty* in a 4 to 3 victory. New Zealand and Switzerland are the only other countries to have won.

The Cup Is Back in the United States
The San Francisco–based, Golden Gate Yacht Club won the thirty-third America's Cup in 2010. The shape and size of their yacht, *USA*, would fit perfectly on a baseball diamond. The yacht has a twenty-story wing sail and was sailed by the BMW Oracle Racing Team. It wound up sweeping the match 2 to 0.

Going for One Championship for Every Lake

The Lakers are so old that they're older than the NBA itself. In fact, the team name "Lakers" wasn't even this franchise's first name. Formed earlier in the same year that the NBA was established, the Lakers got their start up in Michigan as the Detroit Gems. After just a year, they floated over to Minnesota, where they would become the Minneapolis Lakers. Their name, while playing in the Land of 10,000 Lakes, was as appropriate then as it is baffling today. So, why did they keep their name? Who knows, but one guess might be because there was a considerable amount of history in the Lakers name before their Hollywood casting call. As *Minneapolis* Lakers, this franchise netted a total of five NBA titles. That would be enough to rank fourth on the current all-time list.

When it comes to total number of NBA championships, the Los Angeles Lakers have broken out to a firm lead over teams 2 to 32 with sixteen total finals victories, and are pressing the Boston Celtics' crown of seventeen championships.

Brown Out

The current NBA Championship Trophy, the Larry O'Brien Trophy, is actually the NBA's second. The first trophy, given out between 1949 and 1977, was called the Walter A. Brown Trophy. It resembled a miniature Stanley Cup, hockey's top trophy, and it was a temporary prize. The winning team passed it on to the next champs. Even though its design changed to its present form in 1977, its name wasn't changed to the Larry O'Brien Trophy until 1984.

Cowboys and 'Niners

W hen Ben Roethlisberger lofted his touchdown pass to teammate Santonio Holmes in the deepest corner of the end zone, he did much more than lock-up the Steelers' tickets to Disney World. He broke the three-way tie for most Super Bowl victories. Now, the Dallas Cowboys and the San Francisco 49ers are left to duke it out for number two with five championships each.

New owner Jerry Jones fired the legendary Tom Landry (winner of two Super Bowls) in 1989 and hired brash college coach Jimmy Johnson to become the franchise's second-ever head coach. The move worked. Johnson went on to win two more titles. Super Bowl wins aren't the only arena in which Dallas ranks second. They also go for two when it comes to total value. Only the "other" football's Manchester United is a more valuable sports franchise.

The people of San Francisco take extra pride in their 'Niners, because they were the first sports franchise to call San Francisco home. San Francisco's football success derived primarily from the genius that was Bill Walsh. His "west coast" offense and the tree of coaches that learned under him would go on to influence the game to this day.

Super Busts

Some franchises seem to be destined for second. With four Super Bowl loses apiece, the Bills, Broncos, and Vikings hold a three-way tie for second-place finishes in the NFL. Fortunately for Bronco fans, their patience for sitting through four faltering Super Bowls (losing by a combined score of 163 to 50) was rewarded not once, in Super Bowl XXXII, but for a second time the following year in Super Bowl XXXIII.

Pachyderm Polo

Y ou may be more familiar with the kind of polo you play on horseback. The second polo game ever played was on the backs of elephants. Created in Meghauli, Nepal, elephant polo has been around since 1982.

The World Elephant Polo Association Championships have got to be one of the most amazing sporting tournaments on the planet. Teams from all over the world participate: the United Kingdom, India, Hong Kong, Sri Lanka, Thailand, Australia, Scotland, Austria, Iceland, Ireland, and Nepal have sent teams in the past. The game is played with three elephants on a side with the players and their *mahout* (elephant trainer) riding on the backs of their pachyderms.

Participants are in it for more than just the fame and glory that goes along with being a professional elephant polo player. Money from the entry fees is used in supporting health clinics and schools in the communities in which the tournaments are held. Lastly, in a bit of news that has to be too good to be true: the Nepal Olympic Committee has registered Elephant Polo as an Olympic sport and is waiting to hear if it will be in the London 2012 Olympics.

What to Know Before You Play

- The first balls used in the game were soccer balls, but the elephants enjoyed popping them too much.
- Some elephant polo players practice by riding atop jeeps and hitting the polo balls.
- Elephants aren't allowed to pick up the polo balls with their trunks. If they do, the opposing side gets a free shot.

Fox Race

The prize for second most NASCAR wins goes to David Pearson, with 105 wins. Known as the "Fox" and later, the "Silver Fox," during his twenty-seven years of racing, Pearson accomplished nearly everything possible for a NASCAR driver. While second in wins to Richard Petty's 200, Pearson has one record that will likely never be broken: winning three national championships in the four years he raced for them. Pearson has the highest winning percentage (18.29 percent) among all who completed at least 240 races (including Petty). Another record Pearson will probably keep is that he was in the pole position in one out of every five races he competed. Pearson also qualified for an unprecedented eleven consecutive pole positions at Charlotte Motor Speedway between 1973 and 1978. Pearson and Petty had a memorable racing duel in NASCAR's history. It covered such a long period of time that many fans today consider it as the greatest duel of all time. In their prime racing years, the Pearson and Petty duo finished first and second to each other an incredible sixty-three times with Pearson besting thirty-three first-place wins to Petty's thirty.

Two-Way Tie for Third

Third place on the NASCAR winning list is occupied by two racers: Bobby Allison and Darrell Waltrip, each with eighty-four wins. Bobby Allison has been selected as one of the fifty best NASCAR racers. His most famous race was probably the one in which he and his son Davey finished first and second. Darrell Waltrip is a three-time NASCAR Winston Cup winner and 1989 Daytona 500 champ.

199 The Second-Largest Hot Air Balloon Race:

That's a Lot of Hot Air

The annual Albuquerque International Balloon Festival with over 600 colorful balloons launched is the largest hot air balloon race on the planet. The second-largest hot air rally in the world is the Red Rock Balloon Rally, held for the last twenty-nine years in Gallop, New Mexico. The Red Rock Rally limits the number of balloons to 200 because of the limited space in the park. Red Rock Park is filled with massive sandstone bluffs and deep canyons that add to the overall beauty of the race. There are several events scheduled in the Balloon Rally. With some balloons in the air long after the sun goes down, the balloon glow—a firing of balloon burners to illuminate them while they're tied to the ground—is a spectacular nighttime event. How do they know who wins the race? Competitors race to a predetermined location where the ballooner must drop an object onto a designated spot on the ground. First one to hit the spot wins.

What Are Variometers and Thermistors?

The variometer is a sensitive vertical-speed indicator that all hot air balloons have; it measures the relative up-and-down motion of the balloon when it's airborne. The thermistor is an instrument that measures the temperature of the hot air at the top of the balloon and has a "redline" of about 250 to 300 degrees Fahrenheit that warns the pilot when the temperature of the flame is ready for marshmallows and when it's too hot for the balloon.

The Second-Largest Sports Stadium in the World:

Second Stadiums

Holding around 150,000 souls, the Rungrado May Day Stadium in Pyongyang, North Korea, is the largest in the world. The second-largest sports stadium is Saltlake Stadium, outside Calcutta, India. The stadium was built in 1984 and has a seating capacity for 120,000 spectators. This gigantic, three-tiered stadium is also known as Yuva Bharati Krirangen. India's three largest soccer clubs, East Bengal, Mohun Bagan, and Mohammedan Sporting Clubs, play their home games in the Saltlake Stadium. There's such an intensive rivalry between the East Bengal and Mohun Bagan teams that their fans sometimes become violent. The fans of each team have their own traditional way of celebrating a victory. East Bengal fans eat Hilsa fish and the Mohun Bagan fans eat prawns. The stadium is home to the Indian national football team, and many major national tournament games are played in the stadium. When football is not being played, Saltlake Stadium is used for musical concerts, conventions, exhibitions, conferences, and trade shows.

College Math

The third-largest stadium in the world is Beaver Stadium, home of Penn State University's Nittany Lions. It can hold 107,282 fans and is the largest stadium in the western hemisphere. At the time it was built in 1960, it only held 46,284 people. It took several expansions to reach its present capacity. Even though its stated capacity is 107,282, the record for the largest crowd at Beaver Stadium is 110,753.

Fore!

The Golden Bear, Jack Nicklaus, swings in second for the most PGA wins with seventy-three. Nicklaus began playing golf at the age of ten; his professional golfing records include winning the most Masters Tournaments, U.S Opens, and PGA Championships. He won six Masters Titles, four U.S. Opens, three British Opens, and five PGA Championships. Until recently, Nicklaus had won more major championships (20) than any other player in history. Nicklaus holds another unique record: the longest record of winning at least one tournament a year—he did it for seventeen years. One contributing factor to this Bear's success as a golfer was his ability to calmly handle the pressures of the game. Nicklaus was named *Sports Illustrated* 1987 Sportsman of the Year, and several newspaper and magazine sports editors have named him the greatest golfer of the twentieth century. More recently, he has become an elite golf course designer, having planned over 200 courses, including Shoal Creek and Castle Pines. Jack was awarded the Presidential Medal of Freedom in 2005 by President George W. Bush.

The legendary Virginia hillbilly Sam Snead takes first with eighty golfing titles on the PGA Tour.

Tiger Attack

The third most PGA wins goes to Tiger Woods, with sixty-five. Tiger is the highest-paid professional athlete in the world, worth about $110 million in 2008 from his golf winnings and endorsements. Tiger's dad began teaching him how to play golf at an early age, and when he was eight years old, he showed his golfing skill on the *Good Morning America* TV program. At twenty-one, he became the youngest person and first African American to win the U.S. Masters at Augusta.

202 The Second-Largest Winning Margin in a Super Bowl:

Football's Championship Game

The second-largest winning margin in a Super Bowl was 36 points in 1986 when the Chicago Bears mauled the New England Patriots in Super Bowl XX, 46 to 10. The largest was Super Bowl XXIV in 1990 when the San Francisco 49ers beat the Denver Broncos by 45 points. Both games were held in the New Orleans Superdome, with Super Bowl XX outnumbering Super Bowl XXIV in attendance, 73,818 to 72,919. Super Bowl XX also had more TV viewers—92.5 million versus Super Bowl XXIV's 73.8 million viewers.

In the game, the Bears were looking for their first Super Bowl Ring. They were also heavily favored to win since they had lost only one game during the regular season and could unleash the number one ranked defense in the league on its opponents. However, the Patriots got off to the fastest lead in Super Bowl history when Tony Franklin kicked a thirty-six-yard field goal with only 1:19 into the first quarter of play. Too bad it was only worth three points, because the Bears would go on to hold the Pats to the second-fewest yards in Super Bowl history.

Super Bowl Shuffle

The cocky Bears were feeling so good about their winning season that some of the members teamed up to make a rap video entitled the "Super Bowl Shuffle." It would become the first music video by an actual sports team to earn a Grammy nomination. The shuffle became the mantra of Bears fans all over the country, while most opposing fans could barely stand it.

The One-Two Punch

Touchdown! LaDainian Tomlinson heard that call thirty-one times in 2006 when he charged for a total of 186 points. The second-highest scorer in NFL single-season history is Green Bay Packers legendary running back, Paul Hornung. What helped Hornung was that he wasn't just a running back—he was also a place kicker. In fact, 41 of his 176 points came from points after touchdowns, and 15 came from field goals. In total, Hornung only scored 15 touchdowns.

Alexander the Great

The third-highest scorer in one NFL season is Seattle Seahawks running back Shaun Alexander. In 2005, he scored a total of 28 touchdowns (27 rushing, 1 receiving) for 168 points. That same year, Shaun earned the NFL's Most Valuable Player award when he carried the ball for 1,880 yards to go along with his record touchdowns. He was also one of the reasons that the Seahawks went to their only Super Bowl. Shaun wasn't just about firsts, either. One year after setting the single season touchdown record in 2005, LaDainian Tomlinson bumped Alexander to second on the all-time list.

Mustache Mark

The person to win the second most Olympic Gold Medals, with seven, is Mark Spitz. Spitz got his gold at the 1972 Olympics in Munich and was the first Olympic athlete to win seven gold medals in a single Olympics. The most remarkable thing about his medal wins is that each one was won with a record-setting time. Unfortunately, the games would be remembered for something other than Spitz's records. Just hours after Spitz won his last gold medal, Palestinian terrorists took hostage and later murdered eleven Israeli athletes from the Olympic Village.

From 1965 to 1972, Spitz won a total of nine Olympic gold medals—he also won a silver and a bronze to complete his set. He captured thirty-one National Amateur Athletic Union titles and eight NCAA Championships. Spitz went on to set a total of thirty-three world records in swimming, setting his first by the time he was just seventeen. Almost as much as his medals, Spitz is remembered for his mustache, an oddity among swimmers then and now. Mark thought it brought him good luck.

The most medals in swimming at a single Olympics goes to Michael Phelps with eight, which he won at the 2008 games.

Go for the $175!
Olympic medals are designed by the host city's organizing committee. The size requirements are at least .11 inches thick with a diameter of 2.36 inches. Both the gold and silver medals are required to be of 92.5 percent silver, and the gold medal must be covered in exactly .2 ounces of gold. So, if the price of gold is $907 an ounce, then the gold in the medal is worth about $175.

Larry who?

Every true baseball fan knows that Jackie Robinson was the first African American to play Major League Baseball. Yet, very few fans are familiar with the second. Bill Veeck, the eccentric, stunt-crazed owner of the Cleveland Indians, signed Larry Doby eleven weeks after Robinson was signed. The second African American in the majors, Larry was the first to play in the American League. Bill Veeck was probably one of the best baseball owners in the history of the game. When some of Larry's new teammates refused to shake his hand, Veeck saw to it that they didn't come back the next season. Unlike Jackie, who later had African-American teammates, like Roy Campanella and Don Newcomb, Larry was the only African-American player on this team. Larry was a seven-time member of the All-Star Team, twice leading the league in home runs. And his home run in game four against the Boston Braves helped the Cleveland Indians win their last World Series title in 1948. Larry's baseball seconds didn't stop with his playing days. Afterwards, Larry became the second African-American manager in baseball (Frank Robinson was the first) with the Chicago White Sox. Doby's number 14 was retired by the Cleveland Indians in 1994. Larry was voted in to the Baseball Hall of Fame in 1998.

Veeck's Circus

Veeck would go on to own three different Major League franchises, but ran them all according to the same philosophy: "All I ever said is that you can draw more people with a losing team, plus bread and circuses, than with a losing team and a long, still silence."

Stadium of the National Fascist Party?

The first World Cup was held in Uruguay in 1930, with just thirteen teams competing. Four years later, the second World Cup was held in Italy, with the finals held at the Stadium of the National Fascist Party. Dictator Benito Mussolini was instrumental in getting the World Cup because he believed having it in his country would be the perfect platform to promote his fascist propaganda.

Adding a little controversy to the mix, Argentina lost three of its top players to the Italians because they claimed Italian ancestry. One of the Argentine players, Luis Monti, the best defenseman on Argentina's team, went on to become the best defenseman on the Italian team. The reigning champs, Uruguay, didn't participate due to the costs and difficulties of international travel at the time. Italy and Czechoslovakia battled it out in the final, with the Czechs scoring first. But the Italians went on to win the second World Cup with a score of 2 to 1. Italy has gone on to win three more Cups, placing them one behind Brazil for the second most wins.

One Arm, Two Balls
The first World Cup championship game pitted Argentina against Uruguay for the "Victory" Trophy (the first name for the World Cup Trophy). The winning goal was scored in the final minute by Uruguay's Hector Castro, who had lost his arm in a boyhood accident. Another numerical anomaly about this Cup was that two balls were used in the final game. Uruguay picked the ball they wanted to use for the first half, and Argentina picked one in the second half.

Purei Baru!

L enn Haruki Sakata heard that phrase (Japanese for "play ball!") on July 21, 1977, when he became the first Japanese American to be a position player (a player who plays any position other than pitcher) on a Major League Baseball team. Lenn started his career playing infield for the Milwaukee Brewers. The second position player of Asian heritage was Ichiro Suzuki, who plays for the Seattle Mariners, making his debut on April 2, 2001. Ichiro is a hitting machine; he's topped 200 hits in each of his first nine seasons in the Big Leagues. Suzuki broke the eighty-four-year-old single season hit record with 262 in 2004, and he's the only player to reach 2,000 hits in fewer than ten seasons. As a result of his prodigious hitting, Ichiro led the American League with a .350 batting average, received Rookie of the Year honors. In 2001, he was named the American League's Most Valuable Player, and was named the American League's Most Valuable Player. Ichiro was also selected as the Most Valuable Player in the 2007 All-Star Game. When Ichiro isn't spraying balls around the park, he's swiping bases; he stole fifty-six bases in his rookie year—the most for a rookie since 1992. Ichiro is also a nine-time All-Star selection to go along with his nine Golden Gloves.

Beyond Japan

While most of the first Asian ballplayers were from Japan, Korean and Taiwanese players are starting to make their presence known. Korean Shin-Soo Choo is a power-hitting outfielder and budding star for the Cleveland Indians. Chien-Ming Wang and Hong-Chih Kuo, both pitchers, and Chin-lung Hu, a position player, are all from Taiwan.

208 The Second Horse to Run the Kentucky Derby in Less Than Two Minutes:

It's a Shame, Sham

In 1973, Secretariat became the first racehorse to run the Kentucky Derby in under two minutes with a time of 1:59:40. The second horse to break the two-minute barrier was just 2½ lengths behind Secretariat in the same race. A colt named Sham galloped across with an estimated time of 1:59:90 (officials only recorded the first-place time, but later times could be calculated based upon horse lengths).

Sham was in the lead as they rounded the final turn and racing at about 54 feet a second, but Secretariat caught up and won. So, even though being the second-fastest horse to break two minutes at the Kentucky Derby resulted in a second-place finish for Sham, it also made him the second-fastest horse in Kentucky Derby history. Secretariat would go on to win the Triple Crown, and Sham was well on his way to becoming another forgotten second.

The secret to Sham's success? An autopsy after his death revealed his heart weighed 18 pounds—twice the weight of a normal thoroughbred horse.

Paid to Run
The third horse to run the Kentucky Derby in less than two minutes was Monarchos, in 2001. This stud's time of 1:59:97 was also enough to win the Derby. The attendance at the Kentucky Derby was 154,210, which was the second-largest crowd ever at the Derby—and they got to see more history being made because his time was the third best in Derby history. Monarchos's jaunts around the track pulled in $1,720,830 over his career.

From Volunteer to Victor

Thirty-three-year-old Brad Stevens was the second-youngest coach to guide his team to the NCAA Final Four. Thirty-two-year-old Bobby Knight was the youngest. Like Knight's Hoosier team, Stevens's Butler Bulldogs are also from the basketball-crazed state of Indiana. Sadly, the Bulldogs came in second, but had they won, Brad would have been the youngest coach since thirty-one-year-old Branch McCracken's Indiana team won the national championship in 1940.

Stevens got his coaching start as a volunteer assistant on Thad Matta's staff at Butler University. After Matta left Butler, Brad was hired as head coach in 2007, making him the second-youngest college coach in the nation. Coach Stevens won more games in his first three seasons than any coach in major college basketball history. In 2010, the Bulldogs won twenty-four consecutive games before getting to the Final Four.

Quick Grad

The third-youngest coach in NCAA Division I basketball is Josh Pastner, head coach of the Memphis Tigers. Josh has one incredible resume: every year of his thirteen-year college basketball career, from player to staff member to coach, Josh has made it to the NCAA Tournament. Having coached twelve NBA lottery picks, his influence extends beyond the college game. Josh ranks first when it comes to graduating: the two-and-a-half years it took him to graduate was the fastest of any Arizona student athlete.

The 2009 world's second-strongest man was Mariusz Pudzianowski from Poland. Pudzianowski is the only man who has held the title of the World's Strongest Man for five years: 2002, 2003, 2005, 2007, and 2008. Pudzianowski has been lifting weights since he was twelve years old and entered his first competition at seventeen. He's been competing in the strongman competition for eleven years.

Pudzianowski trains by, duh, lifting weights, but he also does extensive cardio routines involving running, swimming, and jumping rope. Six days a week, he spends four to six hours in the gym. He eats a high-protein diet with eggs and sausage for breakfast, pork chops, potatoes, and tomatoes for lunch, and finishes off the day with steak, chicken, sandwiches, and several sweets. His current maxes are dead lift (926 lbs), squat (838 lbs), bench press (617 lbs), and leg press (over a ton). Each year, seven events are selected from a battery of fifteen events for the competition; this prevents the competition from favoring one contestant's strengths over another one. The 2009 events were the Boat Pull, Car Deadlift, Atlas Stones, Apollo's Axle, Plane Pull, Giant Farmers Walk, and Fingal's Fingers. Pudzianowski was narrowly edged out by Lithuania's Zydrunas Savickas.

Strongest Man Events

- In the Pillar of Hercules, athletes compete to hold up two 350-pound pillars.
- In the Giant Farmers Walk, athletes carry two 350-pound weights in each hand while racing across a finish line.
- In the Africa Stone, contestants pick up a stone in the shape of Africa to see who can carry it the farthest.

Breakfast of Champions

The first person to appear on a box of Wheaties breakfast cereal was the legendary baseball player Lou Gehrig in 1934. Later that same year, fellow Hall of Famer Jimmie Foxx became the second athlete to be on a box of Wheaties. But how do their baseball stats measure up? Over their careers, Gehrig outdid Foxx in total hits, RBIs, and consecutive games, but Foxx out-homered Gehrig 534-493. However, Gehrig and Foxx were featured on the *back* of the box and not the front like we see on the Wheaties boxes today. Some others who have graced the Wheaties boxes are Michael Jordan, Mary Lou Retton, John Elway, Walter Patton, and even entire sports teams like the 1980 U.S. Olympic Men's Hockey Team.

Better Eat Your Nutties

In 1924, when a health clinician accidentally spilled a wheat mixture on a hot stove, Wheaties was born. The mixture was tasty and crispy and taken to the Washburn Crosby Company, where the chief miller was able to make a cereal from it. The company sponsored a contest to name the new cereal. The name "Wheaties" beat out "Nutties" and "Gold Medal Wheat Flakes."

The Second Name for Packers Stadium:

Cheeseheads Rule!

What a cheesy name: "City Stadium" was the original name of the stadium the Green Bay Packers call home. The cost of the construction of the stadium was shared by the Packer Corporation and a bond issue floated by the city of Green Bay in 1956. On September 11, 1965, the stadium was rededicated as Lambeau Field in honor of E. L. "Curly" Lambeau, the Packers' founder and first coach of the team who died the previous year. Lambeau Field was acknowledged as the eighth best venue in the world to watch sports by *Sports Illustrated* in 1999. But it was rated the number-one game-day experience in the NFL in 2007 and 2008 by *Sports Illustrated*. Lambeau has the distinction of being the most recognized and coveted of all NFL venues.

The Hottest Ticket for the Coldest Seat
Season tickets for Packers' games have been sold out since 1960—that's 285 consecutive games including the playoffs. The renewal rate for season tickets is 99 percent, and only 192 tickets were for sale in 2009. The season tickets can be transferred to a family member, so they hardly ever go on sale to the public. There are over 81,000 people on the current waiting list, so you better get in line.

213 The Second Most Points Scored in a NBA Game:

Second by 19 Points

Some NBA teams don't even score 100 points in a game, but Wilt Chamberlain did it all by himself on March 2, 1962. The second most points scored were by Kobe Bryant when he knocked out 81 on January 22, 2006. Bryant's Lakers wound up whipping the Toronto Raptors 122 to 104. The Raptors were actually leading 63 to 49 at halftime with 26 of the Lakers points belonging to Kobe. He scored 27 points in the third quarter and 28 in the fourth quarter to end the game with 81 points. Talk about a rebound: earlier that month Kobe scored a season low, 11 points, against the same Raptors.

Bryant enjoyed an outstanding high school basketball career, which he ended with a total of 2,883 points—more than even Wilt Chamberlain's high school point total. At the age of seventeen, Bryant decided to forgo college and entered the NBA draft. He was the thirteenth pick in the 1996 NBA draft by the Charlotte Hornets, but was traded to the Los Angeles Lakers. Since Kobe was only seventeen, his parents had to sign the contract with him.

What's So Great about 81?

- In the 2006 NBA season, teams were held under 81 points 99 times.
- The 2006 Lakers were held to under 81 points four times.
- The lowest scoring NBA game (with a shot-clock) came in 1955 when Boston topped Milwaukee 62 to 57.
- The lowest score of any NBA game was in 1950, when the Fort Wayne Pistons lit up the Lakers 19 to 18.

The NHL Team with the Second Most Wins:

Let's Kick Some Ice!

Across the border from Canada, in Boston, Massachusetts, skates the team with the second most wins, the Boston Bruins. The Bruins have won 2,669 of their 5,632 games from 1925 to 2008. The Bruins are also notable for being the first U.S. NHL expansion franchise. The Montreal Canadiens have won 2,980 of the 5,792 games they've played from 1918 to 2008, making them the NHL's winningest team. But that's to be expected, eh?

The man responsible for getting a professional hockey team stateside was Charles Francis Adams, a Vermont financier of grocery stores. Adams's love of the game started after watching the Stanley Cup Playoffs in Montreal in 1924. Adams hired a great first general manager and former player, Art Ross, to run his team. Hockey's very first African-American player, Willie O'Ree, played for the Bruins during the 1957–1958 season. During their eighty-six years in the NHL, the Bruins have won the Stanley Cup five times.

Zamboni: The Man, the Machine, the Legend

In 2009, Frank Zamboni was inducted into the U.S. Hockey Hall of Fame. Yet Frank never played professional hockey or managed a team. In 1949, Frank invented the world's first self-propelled ice resurfacing machine. The machine is called the Zamboni. Before the Zamboni, workers had to scrape the ice with tractors, remove the shavings, hose down the rink, and then wait for the ice to freeze.

The House That Money Built

T he second-largest stadium goes to the new and (according to many) not-improved Yankee Stadium. Even though this new stadium's playing field has the same dimensions as the original Yankee Stadium, it can seat 52,325 well-heeled fans almost five thousand fewer than the original!

The dimensions of the seats in the new park changed from a width of 18 to 22 inches to a width of 19 to 24 so fans can pack in more ballpark hot dogs. The legroom between the rows increased from 29.5 to 33 to 39 inches in the new stadium. And the ratio of restroom fixtures went from one for every eighty-nine fans to one for every sixty. The main video scoreboard more than doubled from 25 feet by 33 feet to 59 feet high and 101 feet wide and has true HD LED lights. Party suites were not existent in the old Yankee Stadium, but the new stadium has more than 400. As a symbolic gesture, Derek Jeter placed Babe Ruth's 1923 bat that he used in the first game at the old Yankee Stadium over home plate. Did it help? The Yankees lost their first game in the new stadium, but went on to win the World Series.

With room for 56,000 fans, Dodger Stadium leads the majors in ballpark capacity.

The Grass Is Always Greener in Yankee Stadium
The new Yankee Stadium is going green by using biodegradable beverage cups; reducing solid waste by 40 percent by recycling cardboard, glass, plastic, and metals; using lighting fixtures that consume 300 fewer watts than standard fixtures; reducing water consumption by 22 percent with special water conserving toilets; using 100 percent recycled paper; and, most notably, committing to use only 100 percent certified-organic, performance enhancing drugs.

Sneaky Seconds

The second mass-produced sneaker? Check your closet. Chances are you've got a pair. Chuck Taylor All-Stars were the second sneakers to be mass-produced, but that's not where their seconds end. The name, Chuck Taylor All-Stars, is the shoe's second name. When they were first presented to the public in 1917, they were called Converse All-Stars. It wasn't until 1923, when local hoops star and international basketball advocate Chuck Taylor endorsed the shoe, did they become known as "Chucks." They set the shoe standard for basketball shoes for nearly half a century until a company from Oregon swooped in with their "Blazers" basketball shoes in 1972.

These days, Chuck Taylors seem as if they've been engineered to prepare their wearer for a game on the Wii more than a game at the Y. Even still, they are the top-selling basketball shoes of all time.

Earlier in 1917, Keds became the first mass-produced sneaker. It was a pretty simple shoe, with a canvas top and rubber soles.

All Day I Dream about Seconds

It wasn't until the third mass-produced sneakers hit the ground that the athletic shoe went international. In 1924, German Adi Dassler founded a shoe company that would go on to become a leading manufacturer of shoes and style today, Adidas. The Dasslers must have had shoes in their genes because Adi's brother, Rudi, became the second Dassler to start up a multi-million dollar athletic shoe empire. After a fraternal rift that would never be mended, Rudi moved across the river from where his brother's Adidas headquarters sat and began pumping out Puma sneakers.

Almost Out at First

An American League upset over the National League in the first World Series nearly kept a second from ever happening. At the end of the 1904 baseball season, reigning World Series champs the Boston Americans of the American League were poised to defend their title against the New York Giants. But, as Giants' manager John McGraw put it during the 1904 season, "Why should we play this upstart club (Boston), or any other American League team, for any postseason championship? When we clinch the National League pennant, we'll be champions of the only real Major League." So, McGraw, along with owner, John T. Brush, refused to participate in a second World Series . . . at least for a year.

The second World Series was finally played in 1905, with McGraw's Giants beating the Philadelphia A's four games to one. The World Series was played every year for the next eighty-nine years until the players' strike of 1994 shut down the series for what was, hopefully, the first and last time.

A Country Divided

The Civil War wasn't the only thing that divided the United States in the nineteenth century. The country had also become divided about the two professional leagues of its national pastime. In 1903, after much contention as to who was better, the two leagues decided to hold an exhibition between the regular season champions from each league. The American League's Boston Americans wound up shocking the world as they upset (five games to three) the favorite, the Pittsburgh Pirates, in what is recognized by Major League Baseball as baseball's first World Series.

The Second-Longest Sports Program:

Are You Ready for Some Seconds?

The second-longest running TV sports program is Monday Night Football, which began on September 21, 1970. Monday Night Football is probably the smartest (and most successful) move the NFL has ever made outside of the Super Bowl. Imagine living in a time before Monday Night Football. After that last game on Sunday, you'd have to wait a long, football-free, work-filled week before your football cravings could be quenched. Then along came Monday Night Football, and fans had a way to get through their dreaded Mondays.

Monday Night Football wasn't just a television second—it was also a TV pioneer in the way it used slow-motion replay and computer graphics to enhance the games it broadcasted.

The Professional Bowlers Tour has been televised since 1962, making it the longest-running sports program on TV.

Come Together

Ronald Reagan and John Lennon appeared together on a Monday Night Football broadcast on December 9, 1974. At the time, the conservative Reagan was running for governor of California, and Lennon was fighting a deportation order for drug possession. The two were amiably introduced to each other with Reagan explaining to Lennon the way football is played in the United States.

Sumo Seconds

Taiho Koki won a record thirty-two sumo tournaments between 1960 and 1971. Following closely second with thirty-one wins is Chiyonofuji Mitsugu, one of the best-loved personalities in Japan. Chiyonofuji is one of the greatest *yokozunas* (grand champions)—the highest rank in sumo—in recent times and the fifty-eighth *yokozuna* of all time. The word *yokozuna* means "horizonal rope," referring to the same rope the sumo wears around his waist when he enters the ring during the opening ceremony. Chiyonofuji had an incredible career holding the sumo's top rank for ten years from 1981 to 1991. Chiyonofuji holds the record for the most tournament wins in his thirties and even wrestled into his mid-thirties (most recent *yokozunas* retire at around thirty years old). As of 2009, his 1,045 wins in his professional career has yet to be beaten. Chiyonofuji held the record in the top Makuuchi division for nineteen years until January 2010. When one thinks of sumo wrestlers, an image of a very massive man comes to mind—the average sumo weighs 350 pounds—but Chiyonofuji weighed a scant 265 pounds and was one of the lightest *yokozunas* in the past fifty years. Chiyonofuji is nicknamed "The Wolf" for his muscles, his toughness, and the techniques that allowed him to win over larger opponents.

Japanese Imports
Foreign-born wrestlers have been taking over the Emperor's Cup in Japan Championship Sumo matches. Since 2003, foreign-born sumos have won thirty-one of the thirty-eight Emperor's Cups. The Japanese would like a native-born *yokozuna* winner soon.

Vegetarian Vacation

Despite claiming to be a vegetarian like the rest of his family, Major League Eater Bob Shoudt puts his diet in his pocket when eating for fame and fortune. Some of his meat-filled stats: 39 Krystal hamburgers in two minutes, 23.4 pounds of salmon chowder in six minutes, 34.75 pounds of BBQ brisket sandwiches in ten minutes, and 7.9 pounds of Curley's French fries in ten minutes. Unfortunately for Bob, hot dogs must be the toughest meat for him to choke down because in the 2010 Nathan's Famous Fourth of July Hot Dog-Eating Contest, Shoudt packed away only thirty-four dogs, good enough for fifth place. Number one ranked eater Joey Chestnut took first with a stomach-churning fifty-four dogs.

Spidey Seconds

Who finished just ahead of Bob Shoudt in the Nathan's contest? None other than the Black Widow, Korean-American Sonya Thomas. We're not sure how deadly her abilities to consume eighty chicken nuggets in five minutes or sixty-five hard boiled eggs in under seven minutes makes her, but they do make the Black Widow the number one ranked female professional eater in the world.

About the Authors

Matthew Murrie is the second child in his family and has an MA in the Teaching of English from Teachers College, Columbia University. Matthew has nearly a decade of experience teaching and designing curriculums in five countries on three different continents as a public school teacher, private academy instructor, and Peace Corps volunteer. In addition to having coauthored *Every Minute on Earth*, *Guide to the Planet (Planet Earth)*, and *Up Close (Planet Earth)*, Matthew teaches writing as a Visiting Professor of English at Westminster College.

Steve Murrie, also a second child, is a retired science teacher who still substitutes and teaches classes at a local community college and has been teaching for nearly forty years in public and private schools. He holds an MA from Penn State University in Science Education. He is the coauthor of *Every Minute on Earth*, *Guide to the Planet (Planet Earth)*, and *Up Close (Planet Earth)*, all published by Scholastic, Inc.

Index

DAILY BENDER

Want Some More?

Hit up our humor blog, The Daily Bender, to get your fill of all things funny—be it subversive, odd, offbeat, or just plain mean. The Bender editors are there to get you through the day and on your way to happy hour. Whether we're linking to the latest video that made us laugh or calling out (or bullshit on) whatever's happening, we've got what you need for a good laugh.

If you like our book, you'll love our blog. (And if you hated it, "man up" and tell us why.) Visit The Daily Bender for a shot of humor that'll serve you until the bartender can.

Sign up for our newsletter at

www.adamsmedia.com/blog/humor

and download our Top Ten Maxims No Man Should Live Without.